More Heroes, Villains & Victims of

HULL AND THE EAST RIDING

More Heroes, Villains & Victims of

HULL AND THE EAST RIDING

STUART RUSSELL

First published in Great Britain in 2011 by The Derby Books Publishing Company Limited, 3 The Parker Centre, Derby, DE21 4SZ.

ISBN 978-1-85983-985-0
Printed and bound by Melita Press, Malta.

CONTENTS

The stories in this book are all true. All those referred to lived and their exploits are taken from published documentation. In some cases first person accounts have been used to aid narrative.

PREFACE

Every age has its heroes, villains and victims. Some make headlines and engage in exploits which become legendary in the pages of history. Most do not.

This book, like its predecessor, looks at the lives, adventures and times of some of those people, ordinary men and women who found themselves in extraordinary situations.

I have included in this volume some stories which have over the years appeared as articles in various publications and which are now featured alongside much that is new.

Following requests, I have included the detailed account of what became known as the Triple Trawler Tragedy of 1968. The story was originally published in book form under the title *Dark Winter* by *Hull Daily Mail* Publications in 1997.

ONE
Heroes of the northern seas

For their owners the rugged, functional sailing ships of the Hull whaling fleet were a rich source of income. The men who crewed them were tough, resilient seafarers venturing forth to some of the most dangerous seas known to man in order to find and kill some of the biggest creatures on earth.

Like distant water fishing, which many years later would follow in its wake, the whaling industry gave decades of prosperity and work to the port of Hull. It also brought death and disaster.

Hull's whaling industry spanned 70 years, beginning in 1772. The following decades saw 194 ships fitted out and sailing from the port to northern waters.

The hazards were many. Over the years 80 ships were lost, two of them destroyed by fire while at sea and six more captured by enemies of Britain in wartime.

But for many of these sturdy vessels the whaling trade saw repeated trips to the fishing grounds of Greenland and the Davis Straits. *Truelove*, for instance, sailed to those waters 58 times, the first voyage being in 1784, the last in 1852. The *Manchester* made 49 voyages, the *Elizabeth* 43, the *Ellison* 40 and the *Sarah and Elizabeth* 39.

In a paper to the British Association in 1853, Henry Munroe, whose father was a successful Greenland captain, recorded that from 1812 to 1821 inclusive, between 2,000 and 3,000 sailors left Hull each year in the whaling ships and for 40 years the number was above 1,000.

During its 80 years of activity the Hull whaling fleet brought home 171,907 tons of whale oil, an average of 88 tons per ship, per season. It was an impressive performance with this yielding a total of £5,158,080, averaging out each year at £30 per ton, although in 1813 it reached a high of £55.

But while the ship owners and merchants reaped the financial rewards, crews of the whaling ships paid a very different price in injuries and death. This is the story of two of them.

It was a bright day with cloud, but on the bustling quayside few would take notice of the weather as excitement mounted.

On the water of what they called The Dock men swarmed over the moored ships, tough, weather-beaten vessels built to withstand the very worst that nature could throw at them. As they prepared to sail they gave little evidence of what they would bring on their return, not least, according to one writer, 'a savour of a different kind to our notice; blubber when not quite fresh, has a loud smell which could be heard several streets away'.

Back they would come, these adventurers to Greenland and beyond, to be laid up in a corner of the dock for the winter months; heavy, clumsy vessels, their bows strengthened with huge baulks of timber, the whale boats, were stowed upside down on what was described as 'a kind of stage over the deck'.

But that was for the months ahead. On this day the vessels, now fully crewed and provisioned, prepared to depart with huge crowds descending to wave them off in a tearful, emotional and noisy goodbye.

Slowly, methodically, the vessels, each between 300 and 400 tons and carrying between 40 and 50 men and boys, inched their way into the Humber, riding easily along its choppy waters towards the sea. Among them was the whaler *Jane*.

Whaling ships left Hull from what was for many years simply called The Dock as it was the only one in Hull at the time it was opened in 1778. This picture shows it many years later when it was known as Queen's Dock following Queen Victoria's visit in 1854.

A huge roar came from the crowd as the vessels began to depart. Wives and sweethearts sobbed, children waved enthusiastic goodbyes to fathers they saw embarking on a great adventure. Down the river the vessels headed towards Grimsby Roads where the captains decided to lay up for the night. This was a carefully calculated decision. In the emotion of the farewells many men were still drunk. There were also final preparations to complete.

Besides the master and surgeon each ship carried its own experts, among them several classes of officers including harpooners, boat steerers, lancers, line managers and carpenters.

Before approaching the Arctic wastes the vessels called at the Shetland Islands to take on extra crew, ballast and provisions. Then, passing Iceland and Greenland, they moved steadily onwards to the Davis Straits and the Arctic where they eased their way past towering icebergs, sliding silently on becalmed seas, their great wooden hulls pushing an easy path through green, cold waters and into the ice fields.

The first thing sought was a suitable opening or watery lane for the ships to enter. This having been found ropes were thrown out and a number of men left each vessel to help ease her into one of the vast lakes which were the feeding grounds of the white whale.

High above them, the captain of the *Jane* watched the proceedings with a careful, experienced eye. As the boat inched her way forward into the lake the look-out perched precariously in the crow's nest suddenly bawled excitedly as he saw the sea gently part on the starboard bow to reveal the back of their first whale.

On the deck far below the reaction was immediate and frantic. Men raced to lower a boat, clambering aboard it in a state of high excitement. As it touched the water the hands started to row furiously towards the monster now basking on the surface.

In the bow the harpooner was poised for action, gripping the heavy weapon tightly in his right fist, his arm movement blurring as he hurled the harpoon into the animal's side. The whale reacted instantly, in its agony making a desperate attempt to hide below the water, thrashing wildly in its pain, its huge tail lashing at the surface and smashing the water into a creamy foam.

As the monster dived deep the line attached to the harpoon flew down over the edge of the wooden boat, its friction sending up a great cloud of smoke. With the smell of burning wood strong in their nostrils crewmen threw water onto the rope to prevent the boat from catching fire.

For half an hour the whale remained below the surface, dragging the boat along at an often alarming speed as it fought to rid itself of the harpoon. And finally it gave up, rising to the surface in its death throes as more boats raced towards it, the harpooner on each plunging his weapon into its flesh. As the whale died, thrashing wildly as it did so, the waters turned crimson with its blood, the red foam spattering the men as they looked on.

At length, exhausted by its wounds and through the loss of blood, the creature heralded the approach of death by spewing from its blow hole a mixture of blood and mucus and, finally, blood alone. As death came its tail reared and whirled, jerking violently in the crisp air, the noise as it smashed onto the surface of the sea resounding to a distance of two or three miles. Then suddenly there was silence.

The whale rolled onto its back as the reddened waters subsided, the hunters in the boats watching with fascination in detached silence before breaking into loud cheers. The kill had taken a little over 60 minutes.

The whalers then moved in to haul the creature to the ship. It measured some 60ft in length, its mouth 'a cavity as big as a room and capable of containing a merchant's jollyboat of men', according to one witness.

The *Jane* had her first victory. More would follow.

The weeks became months, and the time approached for them to leave, they knew only too well the hazards of an Arctic winter.

Near them were the whalers *Middleton* from Aberdeen and the *Viewforth* of Kirkaldy as well as other Hull ships. As the weather showed signs of deterioration final preparations were made to head for home. But then nature took a hand.

Into the frozen wastes. A dramatic scene in the Arctic with whalers at anchor during a break in fishing operations.

Inexplicably, even the most experienced seamen failed to realise that conditions were changing too rapidly. Within half a day they were surrounded by heavy ice which held each ship in its grip. Sails were useless. They were trapped, unable to move. Men pondered their fate, some praying for deliverance as they gazed across a sea of ice. The whalers were trapped.

And no one on earth could help them.

The ship shuddered violently as the pack ice tightened its terrible grip. Its crew, hungry, cold, dejected and terrified, grabbed what possessions they still had and ran on deck for safety. A northerly wind howled around the vessel, shrieking dismally through its rigging, a shrill and awful sound that brought fresh fears to the sailors.

Despite the desperation of the situation men clung to life, willing themselves to survive and the elements to subside. Men who had never in their lives before prayed now turned to God to appeal for their survival. Among them was an officer on the *Viewforth* who would keep a detailed log of what was to happen in the weeks ahead.

His document reveals a remarkable story of courage and determination in the face of appalling adversity…

1 October 1835. What can we do? Water is nowhere to be seen from the masthead – nothing but a vast body of ice. Came upon a terrible mass of ice higher than our ship's masts and aground in 45 fathoms of water. Here we lay six days and saw a ship in the offing, running down the cant of ice. We could even see the water, and expected to get clear with very little trouble, but how vain are the hopes of man.

My mind is made up for a winter in the Arctic regions. The worst of it is, all the ships are very short of provisions – we are now on one and a half biscuits a day, one half pound of beef and about half a cupful of meal. The cold, too, is intense – the ice on the top of my bed being one fourth of an inch thick.

15 October. We have seen this day a ship from the masthead beset among the loose ice. Three of our men and five from the *Middleton* left to walk over the ice to her, but the distance proved too great and with night coming they were obliged to return. Most of them severely were frost bitten. One of ours was so weak that he had not the power to move his legs and had to be carried on board. The condition of another fellow was most miserable – on his boots being taken off the flesh came with them.

18 October. There was a sermon on board the *Jane*, whose mate is a very religious man. There was a complete turnout from all the ships, probably not fewer than 140.

23 October. Ships covered with snow and just like an iceberg. Indeed, the cold is getting rather alarming – my pillow last night was frozen to the bed. Our breath, I suppose, melts the ice and whenever we rise the frost immediately takes hold of the damp.

We are dangerously situated. Death is constantly before our eyes. Many pray who have never prayed. Many talk of heaven who never thought of such a place.

When I listen to the discourse around it is keen, cutting, penetrating to the very heart. One was talking about his wife and dear little ones, how they pray for us at this time.

Another cried 'Shall we ever get out of here?'

Thus the converse goes on from night to morning the 24 hours around.

9 November. At 4am the ice closed [around the *Jane*] with great vengeance, pressing the ship violently against a berg. Fortunately she was forced astern by which means she escaped the heaviest of the press but not before she was stove under her starboard bow. Ship cracking, breaking and turning up. People running with their bags and blankets, everyone completely stagnated. Dreadful work. Lord preserve us.

15 November. An awful and eventful day. The wind did not take off till 9am and when daylight came what a scene presented itself to our view – the wreck of the *Middleton*. Everyone regarded another in mute despair not knowing it might be our turn next.

Six of our men went over to assist them…one was drowned almost within reach of them. He fell into a hole, the ice met over him and he disappeared for ever.

16 and 17 November. Another man has been drowned. Indeed, we suppose that one half will be dead from cold. The wreck is about three miles from us. The *Middleton's* people have all got on board the *Jane*. They have saved hardly anything.

20 November. Some 50 or 60 men went over from the *Jane* to the wreck. I suppose they would get a good deal of provisions. The weather was fine.

24 November. Thirty of our men set off for the *Jane* at about nine o'clock this morning to assist in getting some of the *Middleton's* stores and though the distance could not exceed four miles we did not reach her until one o'clock. Our journey was the most rugged and dangerous that can well be imagined. Sinking knee deep at every step, clambering over huge masses of ice and sailing over the lanes or openings on broken pieces. Many fell in and narrowly escaped and dreadful were the sufferings of those who were so unfortunate as to get wet.

On reaching the wreck lights were hung out and checks made to see if there were any survivors still around. There was no response. The men spent the night on the ice after having taken provisions which were stored in 15 bags.

Then things became decidedly worse. The diary again takes up the story…

Next morning between eight and nine o'clock, I heard a man hailing us astern. I immediately went to his assistance and found him quite benumbed from the cold and perfectly delirious. He had to be carried on board. I had to do the best I could for him. His feet and all that covered them were frozen into one lump. Having cut away the legs and uppers of his boots, I found it necessary to go through the same operation with the soles and stockings. The latter tore away the flesh from the insensate mass.

So completely frozen were the poor man's feet that when he attempted walking on the deck the sound (I can compare it to nothing else) was like the knocking of a pair of clamps on a wooden floor. When carried to the fire he was not satisfied with being near it, but he actually thrust his feet into the midst of it.

18 December. Ice pressing the ship, shaking and knocking every man up, looking over the side expecting her to go; hearts failing, spirits fainting; human aid of no avail.

Nothing but God can preserve us.

25 December. A heavy press took the ship, which greatly disturbed us for we have prayers every day when the ice permits and this happened just at prayer time. At six the ice eased, but the cold is intense. A very poor Christmas. However, we are thankful we have shelter, for this is a most dreadful place.

27 December. We are solidly frozen up for the present and have been very still for some time. The frost is so severe that even the oil in the lamp freezes and will not burn without being frequently thawed. The ashes, if wet, under the cabin stove soon become a body of ice and the pan, ere it can be emptied, must have a drill to break the ice. How this will all end God only knows…

As the year ended there came a ray of hope, slim maybe, but enough to raise flagging spirits a little.

30 December. Clear weather. Several bears left tracks on the ice. During the dark they had been walking round the ship. At 8pm three bears came close to the ship, two of which we shot and wounded the other. The two were taken on board, skinned, cleaned and hung up in the frosty air to purify. They were a providential God-send, enlivening everyone on board.

But the relief was to prove short-lived. After a decent meal – each man received a pound of bear's flesh to eat – came new horror…

4 January. Twice we have had to leave the ship for our lives and even then it was giving ourselves up to perish in the snow in the course of a few hours.

8 January. Many of our men are complaining mostly of scurvy and some of them are delirious. We got a cask of blubber from the *Jane* three months ago, which we boil for oil for our lamps. If I did not see them eating the fins – pieces of two or three pounds, the very smell of which was enough to sicken one it shows plainly that when a human being has not the means of subsistence he throws off his proper nature and assumes another more savage and desperate.

11 January. Six of our stoutest men are at present laid up and can scarcely move a limb. Whenever they get any help to crawl out of bed they swoon away. Their gums are hanging down separate from their teeth.

19 January. Tremendous hard gales with snow. Necessity drives us to very great extremes for we have been forced to take part of the twixt-deck hatches for fuel for the melting of snow takes a great deal of wood. The snow is very deep; ice heavy all around. No opening whatever. Not a living creature to see.

Deaths continued to rise and men were living at the extremes of endurance. There was no medicine and no proper food to combat the scurvy, which was by now rife. Men prayed in desperation and funeral services became a fact of daily life.

Then – suddenly – came hope, and the miracle they had prayed for so long to happen.

2 February. These few days past are so full of events that I hardly know what to write. We are now in the dark blue sea, escaped from the very jaws of destruction by one of the greatest miracles ever experienced by men in this transistory world. Truly the Lord has made us a way in the sea and a path in the mighty waters. About 30 of our men cannot move a limb.

The deliverance took place on 30 January at 1pm. Since enclosure the *Jane* had drifted nearly 500 miles southward and, taking shiftings into account, probably not fewer than 1,000 miles altogether.

The breezes were strong, and still men continued to suffer and die. But at last they were free and could set a course for safety…

The *Jane* finally returned to civilisation on 13 February after almost one year at sea. It was received 'by manifold demonstrations of joy and kindness'. Men had suffered the most appalling conditions that nature could throw at them.

The story of the *Jane* and her sister ships dramatically highlighted the dangers that whalers endured. But the industry was doomed. By 1870 no more whalers were based in Hull, the last of the great ships being the *Diana*, herself the centre of an amazing adventure when she was trapped in ice from 21 September 1866 until 17 March the following year.

On her final voyage she caught only one fish before a storm overwhelmed her and swept her onto Donna Nook sands at the mouth of the Humber where she broke up in 1869.

TWO

When *Swan* sailed back from the dead

Samuel Cooper was a man to be admired. A short, broad figure with a large head and resolute mouth and chin, he was a local figurehead, a merchant ship-owner and ropemaker in business, an astronomer by choice and a man of science by nature.

He also happened to be wealthy, a fortune built up in Hull and largely based around his impressive fleet of whaling ships, among which one was particularly distinctive because her three masts were green in colour. She was called the *Swan*.

Like other whalers from Hull she had left the Old Dock for northern waters as soon as the weather had allowed. Then came the problem which Cooper had to face for the following two years. The others returned before the harsh Arctic winter set in. The *Swan* did not.

What happened to her would become a part of Hull shipping folklore and was later recalled to members of Cooper's family by a seaman called Richardson.

In 1924 Cooper's grandson, the Revd Samuel Cooper Scott, recorded it in his book *Things That Were…*

'The *Swan* had been away for two years and had long been given up for lost, as these boats could not carry provisions for a long voyage.

'One Sunday morning two men on Hornsea beach at 6am saw a ship in full sail making for the Humber. They took a careful survey of her with a glass and both cried "It's the *Swan*." They took a coach and four into Hull and drove to the owner who lived in Charlotte Street as he was setting out for church.

'"The *Swan*," they said, "will pass Nelson Street (the street looking onto the Humber) at 12 tomorrow."

'"Nonsense," he replied. "The *Swan* is gone with all her crew."

'The people flocked out of the churches and chapel to hear the news and some slept on the pier to secure a place to see the good ship come in.

'The next day the *Swan* sailed in at noon, the captain in the crow's nest, Trinity House boys manning the yards and whalebone hanging from every available place.'

Canon Scott himself witnessed such a scene in the 1840s and told of the hysteria which gripped Hull at the time.

'I noticed a great commotion in the streets, the people running, women with their children in their arms, the boys of Trinity House School in their blue jackets and white ducks.

'They all made for the street leading up to the pier which was crowded with people; others were putting off in boats.

'There, about half a mile off, lay a whaler; the crow's nest (a cask high upon the mast from which a man looked out for the blowing of the whale) was in its place; the huge jawbones of a whale were set up against the foremast reaching nearly to the top.

'Trinity House boys were on board. They ran out upon the yards and cheered. The excitement was intense.

'The whaler had been nipped in the ice and had been kept amongst the icefields throughout the winter and no doubt there were fears she was lost altogether.'

But the days of the whalers were numbered and gas discouraged the use of oil. Although scientists worked to try to make gas from whale oil, they were unable to compete with coal gas.

On the ships chain cables took the place of hemp ropes and the great flat winding ropes made by splicing three ordinary ropes side by side, for which a special machine had been invented, were no longer required, striking a hammer blow at the industries which had made some men rich.

The effects of these and other changes on the whaling industry were to prove catastrophic. In 1834 only eight ships were fitted out, of which six were lost at sea. For the next three years only one or two ships were sent to the whale fisheries, although 1846 saw a revival with 14 vessels, mainly small ones, making the trip.

Government bounties paid to whalers, which had long been an inducement to join the industry, had been abolished by this time. For Hull at least whaling was a dead trade.

THREE
Rise and fall of the 'pirate island'

On the bed of the North Sea, far below the swirling waters that rolled across the mouth of the Humber estuary, the currents began their work.

Tiny particles of shale, rock, sand and stones were moved in a process as old as time itself. Steadily they began to accumulate, gradually building a small accretion that grew large as the decades passed. By the year 1230 it was clearly visible to those who passed by on boats.

In the dangerous currents of the estuary it was perhaps inevitable that a ship would be forced ashore on this remote and lonely place, and this is indeed what happened, the wooden hull becoming a shattered hulk, torn by the wind and the waves. Following the shipwreck came inquisitive men, one taking over the wreck and converting it into a hut. And before long came others.

The island of Ravenser Odd, destined to be rich, powerful and lawless, was born.

One hundred and thirty years later it would cease to exist.

THE HUMBER ESTUARY, 1281

A boat, heavy with cargo, creamed its way lightly across a becalmed North Sea, its sail scarcely filling with the breeze which fluttered gently across the deep green waters.

This small wooden craft with 15 sacks of wool fells and a chest containing silver and gold coins on board was owned by Conrad de Stayne, a Prussian merchant. Its small crew were hard but happy men, busy with their work of keeping the craft on course and oblivious of what was to come.

As night approached a breath of cooler air whispered across these calm and by now more sinister waters. As the hours passed the wind grew in intensity until deep into the night it had become a storm, raging across the open sea, whipping into a frenzy of rage the now huge seas pushing the frail vessel hard towards the English coastline and the Humber estuary in particular.

Terrified, the crew battled to keep the vessel on course, heavy seas washing over them as they clung to anything they could to prevent themselves being swept to their deaths. It was a futile battle and one they knew they were to lose. Their maps gone and unable to hold the vessel on course they knew not where they were now driven.

Then suddenly, without any warning, it happened. The boat was overwhelmed by a single massive wave, vast and uncompromising, its weight smashing down onto the craft, washing away those aboard to be lost for ever.

And so it drifted, broken and helpless, until eventually coming ashore on a small beach, by now quiet after the great storm.

And darkness became day. And the remains of the vessel were found by a man walking the shore of the island known as Ravenser Odd.

The 'tail end' of Yorkshire. The Spurn Peninsula juts out into the North Sea. To the right of this picture in the mouth of the Humber once lay townships and the island of Ravenser Odd. This was how Spurn looked in 1976.

By nightfall the wreck had become the centre of attraction. Many people gathered noisily around to ransack it, carrying away the 15 sacks of wool and the chest containing silver and gold coins.

The wreck later became a primitive home to a hermit who converted it into a hut.

Before long he received his first visitors, fishermen who wanted to dry their nets, sailors and merchants to whom he sold food and drink.

It was the beginning of a remarkable story.

THE HUMBER ESTUARY, 1287

The merchantman, heavy with cargo, made her way laboriously towards Grimsby buffeted by a strong swell and high winds.

It had been a long and difficult journey, but at last they were within sight of their destination. Ashore would be good food, drink and entertainment.

As they neared the Lincolnshire port three vessels sailed towards them, taking positions on either side of the merchantman and guiding her away from Grimsby. Panic began to set in among the crew who shouted to their unwanted escort, but their calls were unheeded.

Steadily the small flotilla proceeded towards a sandy island, on which appeared to be a small town; the merchantman was escorted into the harbour, where she was boarded and told that she could discharge her cargo.

Protests by her captain were ignored, just as they were for every vessel which was brought into the port in this way. Ravenser Odd was building up its trade at the expense of Grimsby. And its rulers were not concerned about the methods they used to enable it to do so.

According to one old document: 'The men go out with their boats onto the high sea where there are ships carrying merchandise and intending to come to Grimsby with their merchandise. The said men hinder these ships and lead them to Ravenser by force when they cannot amicably persuade them to go thither.'

All this was due largely to the influence of one woman – Isabella de Fortibus, the Countess of Albemarle, who was Lady of Ravenser Odd and Lady of Holderness.

Under her 'reign' Grimsby became ever more threatened as Ravenser Odd flourished and in 1275 the Lincolnshire town complained to the king that the new port was posing a very real threat.

She also introduced laws of her own as described in an old document which said: 'They say that Isabella by Robert Hildyard her bailiff, takes toll at Ravenser Odd namely the nets of all ships brought to the land for the purpose of being dried 4d.'

And, it is claimed, the countess was causing harm to other places than Grimsby, among them Hedon.

Not only that, Isabella also set up her own courts in Ravenser Odd. 'They know not by what warrant.'

April 1299

It was, by anyone's reckoning, a town with style. New buildings abounded, ships lined up to unload at its harbour, most of those who lived there were rich, merchants and traders with a sharp eye for making money.

Ravenser Odd, decided Peter de la Mer, was a good place in which to live.

The town was thriving and daily there was more evidence of the fact. This small, some would say insignificant, island in the mouth of the Humber estuary was becoming a port of some renown both in England and abroad. Indeed, it was now a free borough, a right granted by a charter dated 1 April.

As befitted a town of standing Ravenser Odd by now was allowed to hold two markets each week – on Tuesday and Saturday – and an annual fair which began on 7 September. It had its own merchant fleet, court, gallows, prison and several religious properties.

The island's notoriety grew but fortunes were being made and even those who had left the place kept on eye on what was happening there for their own personal gain.

They were rich men who had moved away but who still owned land and leased property on the island. And they returned secretly for one month a year 'for the purpose of gain'.

Their activities concerned fishing, and they went back to take all the profits from these operations not allowing the people of Ravenser Odd to take anything – and refused to pay any contributions towards taxes.

In the North Sea piracy was rife. And on Ravenser Odd discontent began to increase. Even the island's burgesses were not free from corruption: they were accused of conspiring together and making ordinances against the king and his state.

They were also accused of forbidding foreign merchants who wished to sell their wares at their true value to enter the town.

But problems multiplied. General disorder in the town and damage to its quay were bringing trade to a standstill.

3 MAY 1343

'The King demands it – go and see for yourselves.'

The commissioners nodded gravely and started to prepare for their journey north.

Their brief was short and simple – to inquire and certify that the numerous houses built on his land on Ravenser Odd had vanished below the sea.

Land was so badly affected that farmers could no longer make a profit and were unable to pay rent.

By September the Keeper of the Forest beyond the Trent was ordered to have 500 oaks cut and have them delivered to help build quays and other defences.

And so it went on…and on…and on.

By 1346 another inquiry had been held. Men from Ravenser Odd said their town had been so badly affected by the inundations of the sea that most of the soil had been destroyed and carried away.

People had started to move out, too. And those who stayed behind could not pay the necessary dues.

The following year the situation was grave. Two-thirds of the town was wrecked and the town was 'being diminished every day'. Every tide brought fresh dangers and buildings crashed into the waves and were devoured. In the graveyard around the chapel corpses and remains were swept from their resting places and were re-interred at Easington.

As people fled, the looters moved in – 'Sacriligious persons who carried off and alienated certain ornaments of the chapel and disposed of them for their own pleasure,' according to the Abbot of Meaux.

And he warned: 'As with all inferior places and chiefly by the wrongdoing of the sea by its wicked works and piracies, it provoked the wrath of God beyond measure.'

By the early 15th century hardly anything was left. Even the stone-covered path that once led to Ravenser Odd had vanished below the waters. The island, once all powerful, was gone for ever.

FOUR
The peoples' champion

The office was small and untidy. Very untidy. Piles of papers lay across the desk, others were strewn across the floor.

But to Richard Cooke this grubby little room on the first floor of Nos 46 and 47 Whitefriargate was the centre of his world, for it was not only his office, it was his domain, his refuge and his operational base as editor of a weekly paper which combined satire with hard fact.

The *Hull and East Riding Critic* was small in size but big in reputation in the late 19th century, selling an impressive 10,000 copies a week.

It was, claimed Cooke without modesty: 'The smartest, the liveliest and most popular paper in Hull.'

Cooke himself was a man given to a turn of wit, but had a serious outlook too. Many of his articles were concerned with Hull's darker side.

Cooke, who was only 38 years old, was dying and being forced to leave the city to enjoy what remained of his life in warmer climes.

He wrote: '…I certainly need all the encouragement I can get. Physically the crisis has come.'

He had been diagnosed with a heart disease, for which there was at that time no cure, being told that it 'may be fatal in twenty minutes or in twenty years'.

And in a letter which reflected perfectly the dramatic prose of the Victorian age he added: 'There is the terrible uncertainty with the angel of death hovering about you ready to throw his long, bony arm around you and snatch you from your wife and children who require you more than anything else in the world.'

So the days were numbered for the *Critic*. But behind him Cooke left a written legacy which reveals dramatically a city that was most definitely of two sides – those who had and those who had not. Over 120 years later his writings make fascinating, if chilling, reading.

THE SAD, SAD LIFE OF LITTLE ANNIE

A letter to a local newspaper, signed only by the name 'A Sufferer', highlighted the problem which abounded amidst the bustle of central Hull.

It was written in 1885 and expressed concern at what was happening to one of the town's busiest and most prosperous streets.

The letter said: 'I have travelled in all the great cities and towns of this united kingdom, but nowhere have I found so much intolerable beggary and obscenity as in Hull.

'Who that passes through the station gates into Paragon Street has not been importuned by girls and boys for money for bread or a night's lodging or worried beyond patience to buy wax lights?

'If the nuisance ended on this subject nobody would complain, but a refusal in some cases brings down upon you the most obscene and abusive language. I have spoken several times with the shopkeepers in the neighbourhood on this subject and numerous are the instances they mentioned…'

This view was endorsed wholeheartedly by Richard Cooke, who decided to take a look for himself at what was wrong in Paragon Street.

The result was a hard-hitting condemnation of what was going on and what confronted visitors to the town.

Cooke said: 'It is certainly not credible to Hull that bordering the highway from Paragon Street Railway Station there should exist such dens of infamy as have been revealed to the public.

'It is not too much to say that from about 11 o'clock in the morning up to midnight the thoroughfare is an offence in the eyes of all decent minded people. It is more or less perambulated by unfortunates of the most degraded type and whose wretched calling is clearly indicated by their appearance. As the day passes on and the traffic becomes greater so do the numbers of these poor creatures increase also until the scene becomes one which can only be described as disgusting and disgraceful and almost invariably ends in drunken brawls in different parts of the street.

'I do not envy the poor policeman who has Paragon Street for his beat. He has to exercise the utmost forbearance, good temper and tact to keep the footpath clear at all, while at the same time he is powerless to compel those who thus offend public decency to retire to their homes.'

Among those who Cooke found in Paragon Street was a small girl, lonely, afraid, cold and miserable trying to earn a few coppers to keep herself and her ungrateful parents in food. This is her story…

Her name is Annie and today she stands forlorn, selling her newspapers and matches, a tiny, ill-dressed little figure shivering with cold.

She calls out to try to attract the attention of passers-by who may buy from her. Most ignore her, some abuse her, others push or kick her out of their way. Annie is just eight years old.

For her the day begins with a crust of bread pushed at her by a drunken mother in the hovel they call home. Then she goes to work in all weathers, tired and hungry. And no one cares.

On this particular day she is spotted by a tall, well-dressed man who looks with kindness and sympathy on this tired little mite who touches his heart. He is a man well known in the town, a figure of some influence, a man who writes for the newspapers and a man with a social conscience.

Back in his office this man thinks of Annie and the others like her. Saddened and angry at what he sees day after day, he picks up his pen and writes. It is a powerful piece of journalism, one that will be read and yet, like the children themselves, largely ignored.

From the *Hull Critic*: 'Their portion in life appears to be wet, stockingless feet, scanty clothing, harsh words without, harsh words within and never a bit of the sunshine of the world which is so necessary to the healthy growth of childhood. God help the poor little mites! They have none of the necessary and demanding pleasures of childhood.

'People, genteel people whose children are well clothed, well fed and well housed, as a rule, not only speak harshly to the miserable mites, who under

When Richard Cooke ran his publication the Critic *in the 1880s Whitefriargate was a key centre of trade in Hull. This is how it looked in the early years of the 20th century. Whitefriargate was once home to the Hull evening newspaper, the* Hull Daily Mail. *The* Hull Critic, *Richard Cooke's weekly paper, was situated in offices above what is now The Lantern restaurant.*

the laws of humanity have every right to claim them as fellow creatures, but they actually use to them such expletives as they would pretend to be horrified at were they uttered before their own children

'We presume that the general public do not fully grasp the trials that juvenile vendors of literature, matches, flowers etc have to grapple with. The sight of their pinched faces in the streets on a cold night is quite sufficient to bring forth a great amount of commiseration. But the misery of the children does not end with the sleet, the bitter east wind and the cutting night air. After the toils of business most folk go home to a cheerful fire, a hearty meal and a snug bed. Alas, it is by no means so for the wretched little outcasts. Let us give one or two examples of the misery children have to endure.

'We will go up an alley in West Street and turn into a dingy, dirty doorway. We enter a room and see a man in a drunken sleep on an alleged couch. Against a fire grate without a particle of fire in it is also seated in drunken slumber an un-motherly mother, while on the dirty deal table in the centre of the room two cups and a pitcher smelling strongly of beer fill up the picture.

'But there is another figure required to make the scene of wretchedness complete. It is that of the poor wee pinch-faced child we have seen in the street, snarled and cursed at while she was compelled by her drunken parents to go out in the bitter night air for the purpose of earning the means of quenching their fearful thirst. Now she opens the door and in a frightened way – nay terrified manner – enters the room. Her little face is blue with cold and nipped too with hunger no doubt. Her boots are what is commonly termed "out at the toes" and her feet must be as cold as the snow through which she has had to wade.

'Six days a week she has to plod drudgingly along and on the seventh, well she has no decent clothing to appear in. In rags and tatters and doubtless with aching pangs of hunger the child has to wearily drag through the Lord's Day until Monday comes with more wearisome toil and fatigue.'

In a second house Cooke found calm and order, deceptive considering the poverty which blighted the lives of those who lived there. But there was more and, obviously moved by what he found, he wrote:

'Here we see a woman, evidently young, with the mark of death indelibly marked on her features. The place is very neat and one wonders how it is so, seeing the palpable poverty and the ill-health of the poor woman. The reason is soon discovered, however, for scarcely is there time to gaze on the well polished grate before an ill-fed female child enters the room, rushes up to the poor invalid and says how sorry she is that she couldn't sell her papers sooner and so get home earlier (this was twenty minutes to twelve, and the child was a little over eleven).

'Then, in spite of the fearful weather she had encountered without; in spite of the harsh words she had received and in spite of all the cruelties that were

When Cooke left his office and turned right into the town along Whitefriargate he would have passed under this fine structure at Monument Bridge. This was the scene in 1887.

being heaped upon her little head, she bustled about, God bless her, and, weary as she must have been, stood bravely up against her own desire for rest until her suffering mother had been thoroughly attended to.

'Poor little creatures!'

Things began to change in Hull when the Corporation (council) passed a bye-law prohibiting the sale of any goods by children under nine years old after nine o'clock at night. It was a small, but significant, step in the right direction, but before the law of the land was finally changed to prevent such suffering many children were still shamelessly exploited, abused and forced to work on the streets.

Cooke also turned his attention to other infamous areas. The articles were written under the title Hull After Dark and painted a grim portrait of desperation, decay and degredation as the following *Critic* reports show.

FIVE
Vicious Hull at midnight

'Last Sunday morning the peaceable people of Hull who reverently wended their way to the House of God little reckoned of the terrible tragedy that had taken place only a few hours before.

'No 17 Little Queen Street was the place where last Saturday a man was killed. I won't speak ill of him because he is dead, but I will say that it is a pity in the interests of the honour of humanity that the existing members of his class have not before received a similar reward for their actions.

'No epithet is sufficiently strong to express their loathsomeness.

'They wear fine clothes, abundant jewellery and live a sumptuous, though despicable, sneaking, loafing, bullying life at the sacrifice of some poor girl's virtue. Not only that, they are not satisfied with the proceeds of the prostitution of the wretched creatures so they teach them, nay, compel them, to rob the drunken and drugged victim who falls into their clutches.

'No 17 Little Queen Street has in the basement a room about 12ft square. On its walls are hung several oleographs. One represents Romeo and Juliet, another a cavalier and his lady. There is also a picture of a juvenile Cinderella with her broom and many other signs that the web had been made as attractive as the spider could possibly make it. But there is a horrible large patch of human blood on the floor at the foot of the staircase telling how one least prepared for it was instantaneously sent to eternity.

'There will never be anything attractive again about No 17. The murderer was lured to the house in a drunken state and when every effort to get the last farthing of his money by fair means was exhausted, foul measures were resorted to. He was robbed while in a state of stupor. After his purse had been emptied he was told that his absence would be preferable to his company and an attempt was made to bundle him out.

'Unfortunately for him, yet perhaps fortunately for the community at large, the man known as Kelly had a revolver and killed the bully of the house on the spot.

'In his frenzy he shot again and again and, but for powerful arms restraining him, he might have done more good service in the interests of morality. The house and its inmates had long been known to police as one of the worst dens in Hull and my friends in blue make no secret in saying that it is a pity that every bullet of Kelly's six-barrelled revolver had not a hit that awful night. Kelly, I learn from many quarters, is a most inoffensive man and it was only when he was driven like a rat in to a corner that he turned again.'

HOW THE OTHER HALF LIVED

Ropery Street in 1886 was a locality which, even by the greatest stretch of imagination, could not be said to be aristocratic.

Indeed, mused Richard Cooke, most people who had but the slightest regard for the truth would have considerable doubt about terming it even moderately respectable.

While prostitution down there had been fairly successfully tackled by the authorities – 100 years later this was still going on – it 'literally reeked with filth and blackguardism'.

In a dirty alley he came across he came across two 'wretched' rooms where lived what was described as the most notorious family in Hull.

'There are several sons, one with an ear torn off, another with a bridgeless nose, another with a delapidated optic and each and all with some mark of brutal conflict.

'The mother, a miserable looking old hag, is seated on one of the two rickety old chairs in the room, alternately puffing away at a short, black clay pipe and anathematising a filthy old man who is snoring on a rudely improvised couch in the corner.

'Before wooing sweet sleep he has been caressing her with his hob-nailed boots, while in his slumbers he tenderly holds a few locks of her hair he at the same time pulled from her head.

'Her language respecting him is too disgusting for publication and makes a shudder go through us.

'In other tenements similar scenes we witness. In one a brute has thrown the child of a woman with whom he co-habits from the top of the stairs to the bottom, and then kicked the mother after it. All around life is of the lowest order.'

INSIDE A HOUSE OF SIN

Like many other parts of Hull, Queen Street off Blackfriargate was in Cooke's day a grim and crumbling place frequently visited by the police, who were well known to its residents.

Queen Street had certainly seen better times. At one point it was known as Billingsgate, and later as The Butchery, but in 1886 it had become run-down, the home of prostitutes and criminals.

Cooke visited it for his newspaper that year, taking a deep breath before he entered one property, a room which 'showed less poverty than an aversion for cleanliness'.

But it was the woman who caught his eye, a filthy old hag crouched before a meagre fire.

For years she had lived on the 'destruction of the virtue of young girls'.

Cooke wrote: 'Near her is a comparatively young female in a maudlin condition of drunkenness, and with every mark of a vicious life stamped upon her what must one time have been handsome features.

'But the most pitiable sight of all is a young child – a girl of about 11 or 12 years – who unless she soon be rescued from the atmosphere of corruption will in all probability sink as deeply into the mire of infamy as the adults who are with her.'

Down the passage and through another doorway he entered a room at the basement of a rugged flight of steps.

Inside sat a dirty old man, a fat and grimy woman and a couple of young unfortunates.

Of one of them Cooke wrote: 'The girl blushes crimson and bends her head in shame. Only a couple of weeks ago she left the Worsley Street home for fallen girls, seemingly thoroughly repentant and determined to lead a virtuous life.'

And so he travelled on, eventually coming to a place that Cooke realised reflected the fact that the tenant 'did clean up a bit'.

He went on: 'On a neat little iron bedstead with plenty of good wholesome wrapping, sleeps a lad of about 14 years of age and sitting by the fireside is a good, honest looking, respectably dressed young woman, the lad's mother. Surely, we think, there is no vice to be found here. Alas, though, there is. The woman, ostensibly a thrifty wife and happy mother, is an unfortunate and, horrible to think, the sleeping lad is cognisant of her mode of livelihood.

'We get sickened at the fearful atmosphere of sin which pervades the whole place.'

'REEKING WITH FILTHINESS'

Cooke's writings give a dramatic and graphic insight into the way that many Hull people lived in the latter years of the 19th century. In areas which today are sophisticated and stylish once existed appalling slums. Here, Cooke visits one of them in 1886…

'It seems a peculiar thing that vice and crime should be permitted to have its fling under the very nose of law and justice. But so it is in Hull. Within speaking distance of the Police Court places exist reeking with infamous filthiness…

'…We enter one of the houses and first see a dirty old man with limbs as crooked as his heart and mind. For many years he has got a living from the prostitution of women and the illicit sale of drink.

'The licensing laws do not affect his place and the "time gentlemen" of the respectable vendor of alcohol is there an unknown tongue.

'There are several females in the room, some young and some middle aged, but all with dissipation and vice plainly indicated in their soddened features. 'They are the lowest of the low against whom some of the unfortunates of the town appear as angels of light.

'The language of one young woman is most horrible. She is known as Saucy Poll on account of her vile tongue. Every sentence she uses is a disgrace to her sex.

'We cross to the other side of the passage and in a house there find a procuress, her bully and a girl about seventeen or eighteen waiting for a "mark". It is difficult to say which is the most filthy, her tongue or her hands.

'Here is a knock on the door and they let in a respectable looking seaman. Then their bleared eyes brighten up. He is perfectly sober and what is more he will not buy drink from them. He has just returned from the seas and perhaps under the direction of some despicable tout in the service of the procuress has mistaken the place for a respectable lodging house. He soon finds out his error, however, and is given the "key of the street". Had he been drunk nobody would have been so welcome. It would then have been an easy matter to get his six months wages out of him.

'Dozens of poor misguided sailors go to this area after a long voyage and are made intoxicated, filched of their undoubted extremely hard-earned money, assaulted and turned out onto the street without the slightest means of making provision for the next voyage.'

SIX

Murder at the Bull

The name, if not the building, reflects a bygone age. It is that of a public house which stands on one of Hull's busiest roads, a popular hostelry that today is a reminder of times past.

This is the Bull Inn, which was rebuilt early in the 20th century to replace an old building of similar name which had occupied the site.

Originally the Bull (probably once known as the Bell) was a staging post for coaches travelling between Beverley and Hull and the building was thought to have first opened its doors in the late 18th century.

Among those who sampled its hospitality was a traveller who sought shelter there and a waiter who paid a very high price for being in the wrong place at the wrong time.

It had been a long hard day of travelling and as evening drew closer the lone traveller paused, wiped the sweat and grime from his brow and surveyed the landscape ahead of him.

Open land scattered with trees was all he could see. An occasional cottage offered no room for a traveller, and his eventual destination, the town of Hull, was still some miles distant.

As he pondered on how much longer he must travel before being able to find the comfort and warmth of a friendly inn where he could spend the night he became

How an artist saw it. This drawing, which was taken from a volume in the Anecdote Library, shows the finding of the marked coins in the Bull Inn.

suddenly aware of a man approaching him through the gloom. As the rider drew closer the traveller could see he was unrecognisable as he was wearing a mask which hid his features. The realisation was swift. He was about to be robbed.

Afraid, unarmed and quick to realise that he had no chance against a man who was of bigger build, the traveller did what he was asked, parting with his leather purse which contained a large amount of money, twenty guineas no less.

The incident was over in seconds, the highwayman wheeling his horse round and vanishing in the deepening gloom as the traveller stared after him, shocked and trembling as he considered what might have been.

Slowly he remounted his horse and picked his way slowly along the track which served as a road for another two miles before seeing the lights of a building which he noticed bore the sign of the Bull Inn.

The place was warm and the landlord, James Brunell, was a kindly man who offered food and lodgings.

Still badly shaken after his ordeal the man left his travelling bag in his room and made his way to the kitchen to order his supper and to recall his experience, telling staff that when he travelled he always marked his gold coins in a special way in the hope that if robbed he would be able to recognise them and probably help bring the thief to justice.

Supper over, he went up to his room to make ready for bed when a knock on the door revealed Brunell asking if everything was to his liking and then making the surprise declaration that he knew who had robbed him, saying that he believed it to be a waiter at the Bull called John Jennings.

Describing what happened next a Hull newspaper reported:

'(Jennings) had of late been so very full of money at times and so very extravagant that he (Brunell) had many words with him about it and had determined to part with him on account of his conduct being so very suspicious.'

Indeed, that very day he had sent Jennings out to get a guinea changed for him and the man had returned saying he had been unable to do so.

But he was drunk and Mr Brunell sent him to bed with the intention of dismissing him the following day. It was only when he checked the returned coin that he realised it was marked. The one he had given Jennings was not.

Brunell told the travelling man: 'I could not refrain, as an honest man, from coming and giving you information of it.'

The net was closing in on Jennings.

Moments later the door to Jennings' room burst open and a full search began, producing a purse containing 19 guineas, identified by the traveller as his because of the way they were marked.

Jennings protested his innocence but to no avail. He was dragged from the room, arrested and charged.

So strong was the case against Jennings that most of his friends advised him to plead guilty and throw himself on the mercy of the court. This advice he rejected and when arraigned he pleaded not guilty.

But all of this was to no avail. The judge, in summing up, decided he was guilty. The sentence was death.

So it was that John Jennings walked to the gallows, which at that time occupied a site on Pinfold Lane, later known as Waverley Street and today as Great Thornton Street.

Up until the very second of his execution Jennings declared his innocence. His pleas were not heeded.

Within a year Brunell was apprehended following a robbery from a guest at the Bull Inn and at his trial was found guilty and ordered to be executed.

An account of the trial written many years later would say:

'The approach of death brought on repentance and confession. Brunell not only acknowledged that he had been guilty of many highway robberies, but owned himself to have committed the very one for which Jennings had suffered.'

He died on the same gallows as the innocent man he had sent to his death.

SEVEN
High seas adventurer

They were a breed of men apart from the rest, men whose lives were dominated by a lust for adventure and greed. Over the centuries many of their exploits were chronicled, but were later lost to history. Today we can only rely on what historians would later reveal and yet still marvel at what some of them achieved – and at the cost to themselves and others in doing so.

This is the story of one such man, a merchant adventurer from Hull who gave up the possibility of a sedate life in a local business to seek his fortune on the seas of the world. It is a story which at times stretches credulity, but four and a half centuries after it happened there is little chance of proving it to be anything but true. The remarkable adventures of William Cummins were researched and recorded early in the 20th century by the author Walter Wood, on whose writing this story is based.

For William Cummins the great adventure was about to begin.

This young man, of 'robust constitution', had shrugged aside his mother's pleas for him to take up a position as a clerk, a safe and comfortable existence, in his native town of Hull.

Instead, he listened to the stories told him by his uncle, a one-time seafarer who had faced great danger only to escape and create for himself a more reserved existence as a monk.

So it was that William became apprenticed to a well known Hull businessman, the master mariner Thomas Kingsley, who was owner of the *Speedy*, a craft best described as 'schooner-brig'. In 1474 the young man found himself mate of the vessel as she jutted down the Humber and into the North Sea powered by a freshening wind. All looked well and William busied himself with his tasks, enjoying the thrill that the sea could bring.

Not for long, though. While off Heligoland *Speedy* ran into bad weather, high winds whipping the waves into great walls of water which crashed down onto the vessel, which battled bravely but ever more weakly as her boards began to give way under the onslaught.

She sank quickly with scarcely enough time for the crew to launch a boat.

William and a man called Shepherd, an old experienced sailor who had survived such conditions many times before, managed to cling to a spar from their stricken ship and keep themselves afloat until they were picked up by the a vessel called *Tyger*.

And that was a real problem.

For *Tyger*, a well-founded ship, was commanded by Captain Jinks, a man later described as 'a rover of evil reputation'.

This pirate had for years terrorised shipping, scouring the seas for merchant ships and capturing any vessel he could overpower.

But the authorities of the day were determined to destroy him and, with the sole aim of doing just that, sent out two vessels, *Swallow* and *Garland*, both said to be fast sailors, to find him and bring him to justice.

So it was off Land's End they met Jinks head on, a confrontation which was bitter, bloody – and dramatically ended.

Tyger fought bravely, but was no match for the other vessels. Realising his plight, Jinks brought the battle to a swift end, but not before his crew had smashed their way into the spirit room and got drunk.

Incapable of rational thought or action they jumped into boats and shoved off but were soon drowned in a cross sea.

On the *Tyger* one boat remained for Jinks, Cummins and Shepherd, who had remained on board, Jinks for the sole reason that he wanted to leave with a heavy box which he guarded jealously and which he had feared would have been taken by the drunken crew had they realised the fact.

Describing the incident, Walter Wood wrote:

'As the *Swallow* and *Garland* approached, the pirate, who had been below for some time, appeared on deck tugging at his box. Having ordered

Cummins and Shepherd to help him to get it into the only remaining boat, which was drawn up close under the stern, several bags of bread and kegs of spirit, a barrel of water and a compass were lowered. Then the captain told the men to get into the boat as smartly as he did for he had fired a slow-train leading into the powder room and in ten minutes if they were not a good distance from the *Tyger*, they would all be blown to the devil with her.'

The men wasted no time – you didn't trifle with a man like Jinks – but the boat had only managed a few hundred yards when the ship, having a large powder store, blew up with a terrific roar, lighting the sea for miles around.

Jinks looked in from the boat, defiant and revelling in the chaos he had caused. But not for long, because as he celebrated he was hit on the head by a spar blown high into the air by the explosion and killed instantly.

Once again Cummins and Shepherd were lucky and remained unseen by the navy ships. Then, as was traditional at that time, they waited until dawn before casting Jinks overboard, Cummins repeating the Latin prayer for the dead of the Roman Catholic Church.

After some time at sea both men landed at Penzance and eventually returned to Hull and, for Cummins, a new role in life.

Well-to-do now, thanks to the booty which had fallen to him with the loss of Jinks, he decided to go into business for himself and on 8 August 1475 sailed in the *Rainbow*, a two-masted vessel, as captain with a crew of 23 men and boys to search for gold and ivory.

Advice on matters such as what should be taken – items included beads and knives to give to tribesmen – came from Cummins' uncle, the monk who lived in Hull. The voyage soon ran into trouble with a mutinous crew who rebelled when the African coast was reached.

It began with an attempt by one crewman who, believing the captain to be asleep, crept into his cabin intending to murder him with an axe. The attempt failed and the man was hanged the next morning on the yard arm.

But this did not quell the mutiny; a plot was being formed to seize the ship.

Woods takes up the story: 'While ten of the disaffected crew were ashore with Cummins and Shepherd – great quantities of ivory and gold-dust being ready for shipment – and the captain was bargaining peacefully in a tent with the natives the mutineers burst in. There were, however, so many negroes about that they could not reach their victims and two or three of them were stabbed by the infuriated crew. Springing behind some bales of cloth for shelter, Cummins and Shepherd shot two of the assailants dead; two more speedily went down and the rest, dismayed, broke and fled to some neighbouring woods.'

Back on board the assailants were driven below deck, several of them getting injured in the process, and one killed, having started a fire which quickly spread. As the *Rainbow* burned Cummins, Shepherd, six sailors and three boys jumped into the longboat and made for the land.

Their plight was severe, the wreck of their ship was worthless and there appeared little hope of them reaching a friendly coast.

Eventually it was decided that Shepherd and three boys would leave on the chance of reaching Europe and returning with help, their names having been chosen by lot. With them they took 500 ounces of gold dust to buy a suitable boat in which to return.

So Shepherd made it back to Hull and lied about the *Rainbow*'s fate, maintaining that Cummins was dead and choosing to forget about his comrades still awaiting rescue.

But he did not account for the cunning of William Cummins.

After seeing how pirates operated Cummins was prepared for what might happen and secretly gave a message to one of the boys, John Darling, to deliver to the young woman he had married just four weeks before sailing. It was to play a crucial role in what happened next.

Shepherd soon acquired a ship of his own called *Mary Rose* in which he intended to go gold hunting. He did not have sufficient funds to buy her outright and hoped his mother and Cummins's wife would advance him the money. The request was refused.

Darling sent the message to Hull aboard a coaster which was to call at the port and in a covering letter warned that Shepherd was not to be trusted. He was unable to deliver it personally as he was in bed suffering the effects of three weeks' exposure in the longboat before he had been rescued by a whaling ship. Two sailors and one of the boys had died.

The story now begins to stretch the imagination but Wood maintains that the following incidents brought the matter to a close.

He tells us that Shepherd, despairing of raising the money, was approached by 'a handsome young gentleman' who said he was adventurous and wanted to see the world and would put up the money on loan on the condition he could sail on the *Mary Rose* as a passenger.

The offer was accepted.

The vessel sailed on Midsummer Day 1476.

Wood tells us: 'The slim and handsome passenger was Mistress Cummins in disguise. She had taken this romantic means of rejoining and saving her husband and she accomplished both objectives.

'Poetic judgement overtook the faithless Shepherd for he was massacred with other members of the crew of the *Mary Rose* by natives whose women he had maltreated and whose goods he had stolen.

'The voyage home was marked by storm, mutiny and a meeting with a French pirate ship, the *Mogador*. The mutineers captured the *Mary Rose*, which in turn was taken by the *Mogador*.'

Cummins made it back to Hull and went on to become a rich man by trading with the Levant. One of his sons would later command a supply ship which was part of Drake's squadron in the battle with the Spanish Armada.

EIGHT
Heroes, villains and victims

Hull's problems with late-night drinkers are nothing new.

Well over 150 years ago things were much the same as they are today.

One writer in the 19th century said: 'The great bulk of the people were home-keeping folk. To be out at night after half past nine or ten o'clock was considered as most indecorous, not to say disreputable.

'I am dealing with a time when public houses were open until after midnight and there was, unfortunately, never a lack of young bloods and roysterers who had far more money than sense and thought it fine sport and a proper spirit to make the night as hideous as possible.

'I remember when the first gaily bedizened and extensively mirrored café was established in Hull, namely in Little Chariot Street. A party of young

For many a sailor and merchant Hull's Old Harbour played an important role. This was how it looked in 1885. The drawing was by the well-known Hull artist F.S. Smith.

The fortifications of Hull are clearly seen in this fascinating picture. It shows how the town looked in 1603.

men out of pure mischief, smashed every piece of glass in the place. It was a common practice for them and such as they to go about putting out the lamps which they could easily do by shaking the posts.'

WIFE FOR SALE!

On 4 February 1806 bargain hunters got more than they bargained for when they went shopping in Hull.

In the Market Place that day was George Gowthorpe, of Patrington, who sold his wife for 20 guineas and then delivered her in a halter to a man named Houseman.

A newspaper of the day said: 'From their frequency of late years the common people have imbibed an opinion that the proceedings are strictly legal and the bargain binding by law.'

In 1862 a man called Holmes publicly sold his wife at Selby on the steps of the market cross for a pint of ale.

According to the historian James Sheahan 'The woman had been an unfaithful wife and her paramour was the purchaser.

'Some of the rustics of Yorkshire have yet much to learn in the way of civilisation.'

TRAGEDY ON A SUMMER DAY

Wednesday 7 June 1837 was just another peaceful summer's day in Hull.

Shoppers shopped, workers worked and street hawkers tried, often in vain, to encourage people to part with their money.

On the steam packet *Union*, which was lying near the Pier, there was a mood of anticipation of the trip that lay ahead.

The vessel was shortly to leave for Gainsborough to take her passengers to a country fair. It was a perfect day for the event and the trip. One report would later say that the water was smooth 'and the faces of all glowed with cheerfulness in anticipation of a pleasant voyage'.

Then the peace was shattered.

A description of the incident reported: 'The deck of the vessel was shattered to fragments which flew in all directions.

'When the smoke and steam had cleared from the wreck the sight was most appalling. Corpses were strewn around on neighbouring vessels, many wounded and scalded persons were crying aloud for help. Some were struggling in the water and were taken up by the boats which hastened to their rescue.'

Parts of the boiler were said to have fallen 'a considerable distance on shore'.

One man called Matthews was standing near the vessel when she exploded. He was said to have been 'whirled into the air to an immense height and his corpse was found on the top of a warehouse sixty yards from the place where the accident had occurred'.

Thirteen people died in the explosion, some of them were horribly mutilated.

The report of the incident said: 'Some were found sticking fast in the mud at a distance of from 20 to 40 yards from the vessel.'

A second tragedy involving a boat shocked Hull on 8 December 1848.

It was just before 6am. On the small boat travelling down the River Hull near Wincolmlee the 30 or so passengers, all employees of the Kingston Cotton Mills, relaxed, laughing, joking and skylarking with each other.

So boisterous was their behaviour that the boat overturned throwing them all into the water.

One account of the incident said:

'The accident resulted from the disposition of the persons in the crowded boat to frolic.

'The scene which follows fails all description. The men and lads plunged and struggled to reach the shore and the females, void of all self-possession, uttered shrieks which were heard at long distances in every direction.

'Many embraced each other and speedily sank and after a few moments nothing was heard except for a few splashes which only made the silence more awful.

'Hundreds of workmen thronged the shipyards and staithes on the river side but amidst the darkness and consternation which prevailed no effectual help could be rendered. Fourteen people died that morning, eight of them females.'

ORDEAL OF 'UNQUIET WOMEN'

Officially he was known as the Common Officer.

But to most Hull folk this particular official was more commonly referred to as the 'Town's Husband'.

And among his duties was one which brought some a punishment they probably didn't deserve.

This man had the responsibility of providing a 'cucking stool' for the punishment of 'unquiet women'.

The action was an ancient one imposed for minor transgressions.

The culprit was placed in the stool or chair and then immersed over the head and ears in a muddy or foul pond.

According to the historian James Sheahan in his *History of Hull*, published in 1866: 'This machine was exhibited to keep that unruly member, the female tongue, in due subjection, but many instances occur of hardy females who have undauntedly braved the punishment rather than surrender the invaluable privilege which a woman holds most dear.'

Men were spared this, however. They were put in the pillory.

THE LIFESAVER

He is one of Hull's forgotten heroes, a man who served his working life at the city's Royal Infirmary but whose work lives on by helping save lives across the world.

Dr Frank C. Eve was a physician at the hospital from 1906 to 1952 and early in World War Two revealed his newly devised method of artificial respiration, now acknowledged by lifesavers as a highly successful

The way it was. This is how the old Hull Royal Infirmary, where Dr Frank Eve worked, looked in 1890. The building stood in Prospect Street and when built was in an area of meadowland. The infirmary was damaged by bombing in World War Two and closed in the 1960s with the opening of the new infirmary on Anlaby Road. The site is now a shopping centre.

technique which can be used to help victims to keep on breathing indefinitely, without exhausting those administering the treatment.

In the early 1930s Dr Eve came up with the idea of simply tilting a person up and down on a see-saw allowing the diaphragm to move up and down, thus encouraging air to move in and out of the lungs.

The method is effective and simple and requires almost no equipment – even a pile of stones on which a plank can be laid on which the victim lies can be used in an emergency situation.

A more sophisticated way of doing this, however, and one which is widely available, is to use a specially designed machine to carry out the task. These are now found in every intensive care unit and operating theatre in the world.

ELECTIONS WERE 'A FIX'

Today the calling of a general election fails to make much impact among an electorate which is subjected to continual political debate through newspapers, television and radio.

In years past, though, it was a very different story. Election times in Hull brought excitement, heated argument – and corruption.

This came to a head when officials of the House of Commons became increasingly concerned about what they were hearing regarding elections in Hull.

Bribery and corruption on a massive scale at election time was rife, so deeply engrained that a full inquiry had to be held.

Two parties were involved in these illegal activities – the Conservatives and the Liberals – and the scandals that they had created 'from time immemorial' could not be allowed to continue any longer.

The result of this official concern was the setting up of a commission of inquiry which opened at the Mansion House on 23 May 1853.

It was to be a long and complicated affair, lasting 57 days and taking evidence from, among others, all candidates in Hull elections in 1841, 1847 and 1853. In all, 1,200 witnesses were examined.

The findings were shocking, revealing that in 1841 each political party paid 600 or 700 voters for their support. In 1847, 1,200 were bribed and in 1852 out of the 3,983 who voted 1,400 had been bribed.

The final report into all this ran to more than 2,000 pages. Witnesses answered 82,000 questions and the cost to the commission, including printing 1,750 copies of its report for Parliament, was about £5,000.

HOUNDED FOR BEING THEMSELVES

Their only 'crime' was being born with physical deformity.

But in years past that was sufficient for the residents of Hull to bait them unmercifully.

One such innocent was known as Ning-a-Nang, a burly, red-haired hunk of a man noted for his unpleasant smell. It was said he had never been known to have washed himself.

Ning-a-Nang was always to be found around the Pier and earned a meagre living by helping to moor arriving vessels and by scrounging from visitors to the area.

But despite his unfortunate appearance, not to mention smell, he was a quiet man who only became angry when provoked.

He slept wherever he could, but never under a roof, and one morning was found dead under one of the dockside sheds.

It was said he passed away after gorging himself the day before with Eccles cakes, to which some men had treated him to see how many he could eat.

Another well-known character in the 19th century was known as Nut Jack, a small man whose thighs and legs were said to be shaped roughly in the shape of the letter X.

The merciless baiting of such characters certainly surrounded the man described as 'semi-witless' by one writer, but generally known around Hull as Sampson Wide Gob.

This was underlined by passers by who would tell him: 'Sampson, tip us a wide 'un' and, always on the look-out for a fast penny, he would distend his mouth in such a fashion that it was said to appear 'veritably cavernous'.

Then there was Slammy Fox, a very tall man who was exhibited in public houses as a giant, and a 'human nondescript' known as Dockside Nellie who was said to have more the appearance of a man than a woman.

One newspaperman reported: 'Her voice was of the roughest and served to strengthen suspicion, yet she was a woman but unhappily for her a freak of nature.

'She was made the object of a song so coarse and ribald that the sooner it is forgotten the better.'

DANGER AT HULL FAIR

He was known as Old Johnson and by trade he was the owner and operator of a fairground ride.

He was also smart enough to realise that there were plenty of youngsters around who could be easily exploited.

Old Johnson was among those travelling showmen who made their way to Hull Fair in the later years of the 19th century. At that time the annual event, which dates back to 1278, was held on a large piece of square land called Little Dock Green on the Humber Bank.

Then, as now, it was an eagerly awaited and well-attended event, the one-time Hull journalist Henry Corlyon recorded in 1904: 'There was invariably a Richardsonian show or a sideshow (usually in popular parlance termed a penny gaff) and swings and roundabouts galore and what was a never failing source of attraction and pleasure, Wombwell's Menagerie.'

Among the attractions were Johnson's 'high flyers', as his swings were generally known.

He had a staff and was usually helped by his wife. Together they made a less than charming pair. According to Corlyon 'they were coarse in their language and it would be difficult to say which was the more objectionable in speech and manner'.

Yet they were popular, as were their swings, which is where the youngsters came in.

At that time fairground rides did not enjoy the benefits of being steam powered. In their centre was a large substantial pole from which ran spokes connecting to the rim holding the wooden animals and chariots, which in turn held the riders.

Child-power was needed to make the whole thing work and, in return for the promise of free rides, Johnson recruited teams of youngsters.

But they didn't bargain for what they had to endure.

Corlyon wrote: 'If he thought the lads flagged in their exertions he applied his whip to them with unmerciful vigour by way of stimulating their efforts.'

And even if they avoided this, few were said to receive their promised reward.

Others also found a visit to the fair a somewhat disconcerting experience, especially when they saw the dangers posed to roundabout riders by unscrupulous operators.

Hull's annual fair goes back centuries and is today a bigger attraction than ever, bringing in visitors from across the country. This sideshow was just one of the many which attracted interest in the 1926 event.

A visitor in October 1885 by the name of George Augustus later wrote that the event was a 'disgrace to the town' and demand that the powers-that-were made it 'passable and fit for the thousands that patronise our fair'.

Mr Augustus went to the former fairground in St Stephen's Square and described passing down Spring Street, which had oyster and mussel stalls, on his way to the fairground.

Visitors were, he reported, in 'rather dangerous proximity' to shooting galleries near which was a row of newly constructed swinging boats.

'I took particular pains to examine their construction and I may briefly state that although the boats are strongly built the rods with which they are suspended are merely fastened by a half inch bolt and nut, and moreover not one half of the nut is filled by the thread. I write this professionally to my trade as a mechanical engineer and have no hesitation in saying that this is an element of considerable danger and if the borough coroner's services are not called in for this Hull Fair apropos the swing boats I shall be agreeably disappointed.'

He found steam roundabouts, steam boats in motion and steam bicycles before coming to the merry-go-round.

'Here again mothers impress it upon their children to give these roundabouts a wide berth; the horses' legs have a dangerous tendency to strike unthinking children on their craniums and then follows a concussion on the brain, a little coffin, a slow ride, four feet of mother earth and the verdict "accidental death".'

His next port of call was a 'rather pretentious' booth with fishermen and mermaids guarding the portals – 'really not bad specimens of the carver's art. I dare not call them sculptures'.

Then it was on to something equally grand – a yellow bedecked chariot stall on which huge letters proclaimed it to be the abode of the 'Amazon Giantess', who was supposedly 7ft 6in tall.

Mr Augustus went on: 'Passing on our nasal organs are vitiated by an aroma of boiling peas and peering into the various pea saloons we see youngsters of both sexes indulging in a ha'porth of hot peas, never perhaps dreaming if the cook's dish clout boiled with them to add to their flavour.'

TERROR IN THE SKY

It wasn't much of a business, but it kept Blind Arthur in food and the odd drink or two. Everyone knew Arthur, for he was part of the city scenery, a well-known figure who walked the streets with his handcart selling pieces of salt for a penny a time.

He had many customers but when times were quiet Arthur knew how to keep a few pennies coming in by taking out an old accordion and treating the local housewives to a tune or two, his grey beard bobbing up and down to the rhythm as he played.

In between playing and selling his salt on the hot mid-summer afternoon of 24 August 1921 Arthur was chatting with three youngsters, just as he often did, when a sudden commotion broke up the little group as people began shouting and pointing towards the sky.

For there she was, gliding silently high above the streets of Hull, the vast silver hull of the airship *R38*, which had made her maiden voyage just four days earlier, travelling to Howden where air worthiness and acceptance trial and a full conversion into the livery she would carry on service in America was to be made.

Earlier problems with the rudder and elevators had been resolved. *R38* was in good shape for her fourth flight with an intended destination of Pulham in Norfolk.

But low cloud over Norfolk made completion of the flight impossible so the great airship went out over the sea to be put through speed trials before returning to Howden. It was also decided that as there was plenty of daylight remaining, low-altitude rudder tests which would simulate the effects of poor weather over the Atlantic could be carried out.

The sight of this giant of the skies was magnificent and as she made her way over Hull, thousands of people left their homes and workplaces to gaze up at her great silver hull.

This was the scene in the River Humber following the R38 disaster. This picture was issued as a postcard.

Blind Arthur could never have appreciated the scene, but that small group of excited youngsters described it to him in every detail.

They, like many others, would no doubt have noticed creases appear down the envelope, the fore part of the airship rippling like the surface of water whipped by strong wind. She then started to crumble and from the centre came flames, red and yellow flashes of blinding colour which shot skywards.

The great airship, now losing height, drifted slowly and helplessly through the sky, the noise from her engines almost deafening as she passed above the throng gazing upwards towards her.

There then came two massive explosions which broke windows across Hull as the craft fell into the waters of the Humber.

In those few seconds 28 of the 32 Britons aboard the *R38* died, as did 16 of the 17 Americans. Five crew members who had been in the tail section survived.

But things could have been worse, very much worse, had it not been for the fast thinking and courage of one man. He was the *R38*'s commanding officer, Flt-Lt Wan, and is thought to have steered the giant craft away from the city centre to prevent even greater horror.

Although horrifically burned about the head, injuries from which he later died in Hull Royal Infirmary, the officer was able to tell how the whole drama ended in just a few seconds. The *Hull Daily Mail* of Thursday 25 August reported: 'The airship had slowed down from 64 to 50 knots an hour and they were approaching the Humber when the disaster happened.

'There was a sudden crack and I thought several girders had cracked. Almost immediately there was a terrific explosion.

'He thought that most of the crew had been killed in that explosion. He remained in the fore car until the wreckage almost touched the water when he jumped out and became fastened in the remains of the craft.'

Mr Harry Bateman, scientific assistant of the National Physical Laboratory, was among the survivors.

He told the newspaper: 'We had reached 60 knots per hour, which was the specified speed to be attained and had cut down just prior to the disaster to between 45 and 50 knots.

The plaque which is the centrepiece of the memorial in Hull's Western Cemetery.

A tribute to those who died. This is the memorial created in Hull's Western Cemetery for the victims of the R38 disaster. The names of those who lost their lives are remembered in the two plaques on either side of the memorial.

'The engine was firing evenly. Rudder controls were being tested when suddenly there were a number of jars and in a few seconds several of the girders snapped and the airship broke in two.

'We dipped at a terrible angle and I realised we were done. I was in the rear portion that appeared to float before descending slowly and as I sat in the cockpit in the tail I saw the smoke from the foremost portion of the wreckage above Hull.

'I had been in the tail the whole time of the speed tests and we were about 1500 feet up.'

Some of the 16 Americans killed in the disaster were taken home for burial, others lie in Elloughton churchyard.

In Hull a plaque was fixed in the Western Cemetery where nine of the British victims are buried, but it was later stolen. However, a handsome memorial to the victims remains to commemorate that terrible day.

NINE

Hull's first lady of fashion

The showroom was impressively large and expensively decorated. It had to be, for only the best people visited this exclusive establishment. Indeed, only the best people, the monied women whose husbands ran Hull, could afford to walk through its door.

It was a room which impressed and that was exactly what its creator intended it to do; its visitors stepped in from Kingston Square onto a deep, rich crimson velvet carpet.

The magazine *Hull Lady*, whose title aptly summed up its readership, said of this room in 1901 that it displayed 'the choicest and most unique gowns, dress fabrics, trimmings etc for day and evening wear'.

In particular the magazine writer was impressed with a French model gown in black velvet, handsomely embroidered with ecru lace applique, and a princess robe in blue Orient satin, charmingly trimmed with blue mousseline de sole.

'Here were also several lovely evening cloaks, but which especially took my attention was in banana coloured cloth, with a beautiful muslin collar and necklet of ermine.'

Style indeed, but then that was what this place was all about. And for years it remained THE most exclusive dress emporium in Hull and far beyond.

It stood at Nos 1 and 2 Kingston Square and was the base of Madam Clapham, Hull's first lady of fashion, a remarkable woman who was to achieve international fame for her fabulous dress designs.

Not bad for someone once said to be 'a little nobody with neither education nor background'.

It all began when the young Miss Emily MacVitie started work at a dressmaking firm in Scarborough, her job being to pick up dropped pins from the floorboards. Hardly the most auspicious start to what would prove a

The name above the door tells its own story. This was once the premises of Madame Clapham in Kingston Square, Hull. It is now a hotel.

dazzling career in which she would be regarded as the definitive voice on ladies' fashion.

Emily was ambitious and after marrying Haigh Clapham, a clerk from Wakefield, she moved to Hull where the couple, after careful deliberation, decided to invest all their savings in a house at No. 1 Kingston Square from which to run her business. From the start she appreciated the competition was tough – at the time Hull had more than 200 established costumiers – but she was determined to build on her talents and ambitions.

The salon opened in 1887 and within three years Madam Clapham, as she soon became known, was acknowledged as the smartest of the Hull dressmakers. Within five years of opening she was said to be 'good enough for London'.

But that was not what she wanted. For despite her success Madam Clapham was determined to remain provincial, hating advertising and publicity and determined to remain away from the fashion centres of the capital and of Paris.

But her reputation grew and after two of the great beauties of the time – Muriel Wilson and her sister – wore Madam Clapham clothes when in London orders began to arrive.

By 1901 she was making so many white dresses for debutantes to wear at court that she was able to described herself as 'Court Dressmaker'.

So fast was the rise of her business that by the turn of the century Madam Clapham employed about 150 girls at Kingston Square, the buildings being divided into bodice rooms, skirt rooms, coat and sleeve rooms and an embroidery room.

All sections of the business were highly specialised and a girl taken on in a particular area would remain there until she left employment, Madam Clapham, a great believer in specialisation, taught her girls that it was better to excel in one aspect of dressmaking than to have general, all-round knowledge.

Each workroom was controlled by a fitter who was ultimately responsible for the cutting of garments and fitting them on a client. Seamstresses were very much background workers, not being allowed to enter the showroom and never having contact with the ladies they dressed.

Apprentices were taken on and spent their first year under the supervision of trained seamstresses doing simple, tedious jobs.

The embroidery room was fitted with frames at which sat seamstresses who sewed intricate designs first drawn onto tissue paper. Transfers were never used.

The hours were long and the work had to be of the highest standard. Girls and women would start at 8.30am and work through until 6.30pm on weekdays. On Saturdays, too, the workrooms were busy, with staff working from 8.30am until 1pm. And discipline was strict. The door was bolted each day at 9am. Anyone arriving later was marked absent.

Conditions of employment included girls facing the prospect of three 'notice' nights a week on which Madam Clapham could order them to work extra hours to complete urgent orders. There was no overtime.

From time to time such working practices contravened the law, the Factory Acts stating that girls aged under 18 must not work after 9pm and that girls under 16 must not work late at all. Such regulations did not worry Madam Clapham and when factory inspectors called, younger staff members were hidden in wardrobes.

Girls were paid according to their age and experience. Before 1900 they worked the first year of their apprenticeship for no wages at all and pay was generally low. But working in the establishment was a prestigious job and despite the wages Madam Clapham was never short of applicants, conducting all interviews herself and making family background, above merit in needlework, her priority in selecting staff.

Working conditions were spartan, with the girls sitting at a central table on stools. Floorboards were bare and in winter the rooms were said to be bitterly cold.

This was not a place in which Madam Clapham herself was often seen, preferring as she did to remain in the showroom to meet her clients and apart from the fitters most employees saw her only at the time of their engagement and dismissal.

As her business, not to mention her fame, grew Madam Clapham began to attract the attention of fashion-conscious women in other countries. Among these was Queen Maud of Norway.

Queen Maud was very impressed. The gown she saw was beautifully made, stylish and colourful, its exquisite embroidery and needlework a tribute to the skill of its creators.

It was, she decided, work of the highest order, exactly what a queen should be seen in.

Inquiries were made by the royal household. And to Madam Clapham, of Hull, came a client who would be dressed by her for the rest of her life.

It was after Madam Clapham spent a week in London that she was summoned by telephone to Appleton House at Sandringham to show Queen Maud a selection of her gowns. The result was that every year afterwards the couple met in the Spring and Autumn either at Appleton House or Claridges Hotel, the queen usually ordering several gowns.

As with all garments produced by Madam Clapham they were sewn in Hull, the seamstresses often using the Queen's own trimmings of lace or fur. The dresses were fitted on a model which was an exact replica of the queen's shape.

So close did the couple become that Mr and Mrs Clapham once made the journey to Norway as guests of Queen Maud.

Meanwhile, the business continued to expand and space at No. 1 became so short that expansion was a necessity, Madam Clapham bought the premises next door and eventually the house next door to that too, the deal being struck shortly before the outbreak of World War One.

But while Hull continued to be the major showpiece for her creations she also held court in other towns, taking suites of rooms at places such as the Royal Station Hotels in Harrogate, York and Grimsby and at the Mendeville Hotel off Oxford Street, London.

And high society loved it. As her name became ever more famous demand for her designs increased, ladies across the country were wearing her clothes at house parties, race meetings, fêtes, musical evenings, dinner parties and balls. And for any respectable bride a Madam Clapham wedding gown was a necessity.

But then came the war. And with it came a blow to the business.

Although fabric supplies were not affected by the conflict, and while social life around the country, particularly so far as the gentry was concerned, carried on more or less as normal, many of her patrons turned to helping with the war effort. Nurses' uniforms began to take the place of tea gowns.

Things would never be quite the same again. And after the conflict young ladies began to dress less elegantly, moving away from the elaborate and extravagant dresses favoured by their mothers for a style that required much less fabric and sewing. Through the 1920s and 1930s the business declined, Madam Clapham not being favoured by the young and as a result was catering for a decreasing number of older women.

Then came World War Two which was to cause the near collapse of the salon in Hull with many employees being laid off when fabrics became scarce and rationing was introduced.

But the business did survive and after the war Madam Clapham was again able to supply her devoted and ageing customers with outfits for their society balls and race meetings.

Things would, however, never again reach the peak they did in the heady days of the early 20th century.

In January 1952 Madam Clapham died at the age of 96, leaving £28,000. Her home in Cottingham and Nos 1 and 2 Kingston Square were sold. Her niece continued to work as a dressmaker at No. 3 until 1967.

TEN
Scandal of the passports from Hell

They were conmen who saw easy pickings the day they came to Hull. And the innocent townsfolk soon fell for the smooth talk of men who were out to make a fast and easy buck. This is their story.

My name is Ludovick Muggleton. Hardly an easy one to remember, but it got me by well enough. Helped make me quite well known in fact, although as it turned out not the sort of fame that I would probably have gone out looking to achieve.

But that is enough of that for the moment. Who, you may well ask, am I?

To put it simply, my friends, I am by trade a working tailor although I now regard myself as more a man of business, a man who likes a little luxury in life, a man who knows how to make a few pounds the easy way. For that, though, I rely on the help of my great friend and brother-in-law, Sandy Reeve.

It was in 1657 when we finally arrived in your town of Hull and a pleasant experience it was, too. To start with there were the imposing fortifications on the top of which grew the Common Pink 'in great plenty'.

The River Hull or Old Harbour where shipping was berthed extended to what is now North Bridge, where a bridge was built and chains were drawn over the entrance at night for the safety of shipping.

On the west bank of the river were wharves or staithes and warehouses. The opposite side was occupied by the garrison and blockhouses.

High (or Hull) Street followed the line of the river after the Danish custom and here were also the houses of leading merchants.

Numerous lanes branched off High Street in herringbone fashion to Market Place and Lowgate.

Gardens ran along inside the walls from Beverley Gate to Hessle Gate and gentlemen's houses had large open spaces or garden plots. Blackfriargate and Blanket Row (then known as Monkgate) contained the houses of prominent townspeople.

The population numbered not more than 4,000 or 5,000, who relied largely upon the port's overseas trade for a livelihood and during the sieges of Hull locally owned ships carried on an extensive trade with countries in Europe.

Certainly I found a town where life could hardly be said to be easy for the local people.

Mail was carried to London once a week and received in return once a week. It was taken on horseback after being taken across the Humber to Barton. The route went via Brigg, Lincoln and Peterborough. Communications were difficult and most Hull people did not travel beyond a few miles or risk the unwelcome attention of footpads and highwaymen.

York was far afield and London foreign. The advantage Hull people had was water transport by wherries up the Humber and the Trent and Ouse and across by the Hull and Barton ferry.

Country people from the East Riding and North Lincolnshire came into town on market days –Tuesdays and Saturdays.

Mariners, an important part of the population, were united under the aegis of Trinity House, which looked after their interests on both land and sea.

Apart from the Grammar School there were few facilities for education and the majority were not troubled with instruction of even the most elementary kind. Few could read or write.

Recreations were few and apart from religious activities and social meetings at the inns there was little to occupy the people outside their own homes.

Hull Fair was an institution, so also was the annual production of the mystery play by the Mariners' Guild. Bowling was a popular pastime.

There were no newspapers and people for their knowledge of happenings in the outside world had to rely on the newsletters which arrived once a week and were eagerly scanned and discussed in the places where men were wont to gather, notably the licensed houses of which there were four – the King's Head on High Street, the White Horse in the Market Place, the Whitefriars Hotel in Market Place and the George and Dragon in George Yard.

But we as visitors particular enjoyed the ambience of the place, not to mention that strong ale which you brewed there.

The name of some of it, I recall, was Hull Cheese. It was described to me thus: 'Hull Cheese is much like a loaf out of a butcher's basket. It is composed of two simples, malt and water, in one compound and is cousin germaine to the mightiest ale in England.' Someone else told me that to have 'eaten' Hull Cheese simply meant that you were drunk.

So it was that on our arrival we went, as advised, to the King's Head Inn in that most pleasant area of town called High Street to sample some of this magnificent brew.

A grand old building, this. One of the oldest in the town, I believe, a place where reigning monarchs had stayed in fine apartments. It also happened to be the point where the first stage coach left the town, a point I noted with interest should the need arrive for a swift departure.

We found the rooms as good as any we had stayed in and believe me we had slept in many as we travelled across the country, mostly finding ourselves among less salubrious company in the various pothouses that seemed to litter town after town.

The King's Head, though, was different. It clung onto a reputation of finesse, although when we arrived that summer it certainly appeared to have seen better times.

Well, we sampled your ale and passed our message on to those assembled there and found them keen to listen to what we had to say.

A successful start indeed to our little exercise, the results of which were very pleasing as we would find out a few days later.

The religious life of the nation was changing. Protestantism and non-conformity were coming to the fore, a change characterised by confusion and chaos both incredible and indescribable.

The religious life of England was in a state of flux and the circumstances gave rise to the arrival of new religious sects by the dozen. The gate was open to adventurers, charlatans and imposters.

Among them were men like Muggleton and Reeve. Muggleton was said to be wholly devoid of education, but had a bright and cunning mind. In the pothouses and hotels across the country he proclaimed against those who refused to believe in his religious testimony. This included a declaration that the Supreme Being was only 6ft in height and that the sun was only four miles from the earth…

This, audiences were convincingly assured, was reality. And the men before them were also assured because Muggleton and Reeve were 'the two last witnesses of God the Almighty ever to be appointed on earth'.

It was a message they were supremely adept at putting across. And in Hull they found audiences just as willing to hear and believe them as anywhere else…

MUGGLETON'S STORY

Well, we sampled the ale, slept in large and comfortable beds and then set to work. First we placed large placards across Hull notifying the public that they were about to meet prophets who would stagger the population and make their hair stand on end. We told them we could save them from or condemn them to eternal punishment. And they believed us.

For a meeting place we chose Thomas Ferries' house at the corner of Whitefriargate and Trinity House Lane. We charged people to come in, of course – front seats a shilling, second seats sixpence and side seats threepence.

It was December but the fact that snow was falling made no difference to the turnout. They just could not wait to hear us. The Market Place and round into Silver Street were crowded with people queuing to hear us prophets.

The scenes were truly amazing, but I will leave the town alderman John Symons to describe what happened.

EYEWITNESS: JOHN SYMONS

Chaos ensued when the doors opened and once we all managed to get inside we saw that the rostrum was nothing more than three boards fixed on two trestles. Muggleton asked us to join him in prayer and Reeves moved around the packed gathering with plates of bread and two large pitchers filled with water. He had little to say throughout the whole proceedings apart from 'Amen.'

Muggleton told them he had a vision and that the Almighty had suffered in death, leaving him and Brother Reeve as executors. Their duty was to elect all those whom they considered fit to enter the Kingdom of Heaven and consign the others to the eternal pit, there to be beaten and burned with red-hot fire and brimstone.

MUGGLETON'S STORY

Well, that's what we told them and they really wanted to hear it all. Then came the rub. We offered them advice on how to redeem themselves by offering prayers for two days and then to bring to us or our appointees the sum of two broad pieces (gold coins worth 25 shillings each) in aid of furnishing them with the means of washing them clean from their sins and wickedness. A sort of passport from Hell, if you like.

It was a profitable exercise, netting us a handsome £300 in just five days.

We decided to leave when attendances at the meetings began to fade away. As we left we thought we'd give it a few more months and then we'd be back.

When all this began I was 50 years old. The idea just came to me one day and I thought I'd give it a try. It also brought me a lot of attention from women, although the authorities took a dim view of what was going on, deciding eventually to put a stop to what they considered to be blasphemous proceedings.

From Hull Muggleton and Reeve continued their journey, pulling the same confidence trick in town after town. The law was catching up, although it took 20 years for it to do so.

Eventually, on 26 January 1677, Ludovick Muggleton went on trial at the Old Bailey and was sentenced to stand in the pillory for three days in several parts of London. He was also fined £500 or to be kept in jail if he failed to pay.

Muggleton was sentenced by the infamous Judge Jeffries. In the pillory he was almost killed by the brickbats thrown at him.

But he survived and lived until he was 90 years old, for several years retaining many of his followers who, as a sect, were known as…The Muggletons.

ELEVEN
Victims of a city at war

Mention the Blitz of World War Two and certain places always come to the fore – London, Coventry, Liverpool.

Yet one other city which was bombed, and bombed more comprehensively than most others, is rarely mentioned. It was Hull, said by some to be the second most devastated city after London during the entire war.

Hull suffered its ordeal with fortitude and dignity.

During bombing raids about 1,200 people died and another 3,000 were injured.

A total of 87,715 houses were damaged, only 5,945 did not suffer the effects of the bombing raids.

And in 815 alerts Hull people spent 1,000 hours wondering where the next bomb would fall.

Across the city families sought the safety of air raid shelters, but 250 domestic shelters and 120 which were used for communal purposes were destroyed, although more than 800 people were saved after being trapped.

A tribute to the people of Hull came from Sir William Bartholemew, Regional Commissioner for the North Eastern Region 1941 to 1945. Writing in T. Geraghty's book *A North East Coast Town, Ordeal and Triumph* he said:

'Never once, even during the long period when German bombs fell almost daily and still more frequently at night, did the citizens waver in their determination to see it through and to keep the city, its port and its factories in full activity.

'...Many citizens, men, women and children, forfeited their lives or were terribly injured, but their fellow citizens stood firm. The wonderful women were undaunted and kept their homes going, often in conditions which had to be seen to be believed.

'I have seen the city with great fires raging in many places and devastation widespread, but the ideal of its people throughout was defiance, often expressed in best Yorkshire amid scenes of ruin and fire.'

Here we take a look at how local people faced up to the dangers of just some of the nights of terror when the Luftwaffe brought death and devastation.

LAST RAID OF THE WAR

Within weeks the war would be over.

Across Europe the Nazis were being overwhelmed as Allied forces relentlessly advanced towards Berlin.

In Hull, as in other cities, people had begun to pick up their shattered lives. The devastating air raids had ceased, but the results of the bombing had taken a massive toll.

Despite this, though, there was a feeling of optimism. And – at long last – a realisation that life could begin again.

But in Europe there remained among Hitler's fanatics a determination to fight on against all the odds. And that included the Luftwaffe, which, although almost totally destroyed, showed it still believed the cause was worth fighting for.

And so it was that on a Saturday night in Hull, as hundreds of people began to leave cinemas to make their way home, the Germans struck for the last time a city which had seen more than its share of bombing raids.

As cinema-goers waited for buses or walked the pavements of Holderness Road an enemy plane swooped low above them dropping containers of small fragmentation bombs. They fell onto a road, crowded by now with pedestrians and traffic, killing 12 people and seriously injuring 22 more.

Hull's last bombing raid of World War Two came on 17 March 1945. It was officially said to have caused only superficial damage to shops and houses.

The *Hull Daily Mail* reported the incident, but was still subject to wartime reporting restrictions which meant that Hull could only be referred to as a north-east town. Similarly, little clue was given to exact locations. The book *A North East Coast Town*, which told the story of bombing raids on Hull, later disclosed that the raid of 17 March affected Holderness Road, Morrill Street and Holland Street.

Describing the scene following the raid the paper said: 'Quite close to the incident is a first aid post, but unfortunately this was closed and none of the personnel were on duty. The injured were taken to another casualty post.

'One of the injured was a prominent local British Legion official who was travelling in a motor car. A bomb exploded at the rear of the car and he received shrapnel wounds in the thigh and behind the ear. The driver suffered from flying glass. A bus carrying a full load of passengers pulled up and escaped damage and none of the passengers were injured.'

The paper went on: 'A local Press photographer was travelling in his car when he saw a flash in the sky followed by the noise of several explosions. Later he came across inert figures lying in the road and gave valuable assistance by taking injured children to the casualty post.'

The paper told the story of a Mr and Mrs Martin who were returning home from a club where they had made arrangements for a concert to be held in aid of a war comforts fund.

An amateur tenor vocalist, Mr Martin and his brother were known as the Martin brothers and he had just composed a popular song – *Just Tell Me The Truth*.

He and his wife were walking arm-in-arm when the bombs hit.

The *Mail* said: 'Their son left a cinema to return home and travelled by bus. As he reached the corner of the street the bombs exploded and he ran into a shelter for safety. He afterwards learned the fate of his parents who, according to family calculations, must have been only a short distance away from him when they were killed.'

Mr Martin, a lorry driver, was a member of a rescue squad and drove in London during the capital's daylight bombing, carrying supplies to hospitals.

Another victim was Mr John Reed (71), a retired docker who lost his life while trying to protect a boy. The paper said: 'Running from his house, he was crossing a side street when there was a burst of shrapnel. He flung himself on the boy. Both fell and were killed.'

Mr Stanley Duncan (21), formerly a clerk in the medical officer's department and home on leave after receiving a commission, was fatally injured.

A mother of month-old twins also died, as did Mr Walter Coggle (60), Mr James Ollenshaw (49), two boys aged 12 and a girl aged two.

The *Hull Daily Mail* said: 'The injured included children aged eight to 16. Mrs Lilian Winter was taken to hospital and her two-year-old child was treated at a first aid post.

'Herbert Thorsden, who with his wife was injured by shrapnel and taken to hospital, was a member of Home Guard rifle club.'

The following day repair squads were out carrying out work on shops and houses.

The paper added: 'Armed with mops and pails women in some terraces were swilling throughout the morning.'

CITY BURNED BUT WAS NOT BEATEN

The writer of this graphic account of a night of hell in Hull is unknown.

It was printed several years ago and signed: 'Anonymous…in memory of the dead and the bombed out and the crippled of body and mind.'

Outdoors, under a bright half moon, engines whine and balloons silently slip up to alert altitude. They are expecting visitors.

Just after supper the sirens wail. Soon, a rumbling of guns – way off.

Windows rattle. Over my shoulder. Tiger the she-cat – ears pricking – takes cover behind the great marble clock on the mantelpiece.

Out at the front I stare between the gables over city and docks, the half moon riding high under a fine May night.

A faint smell of freshly clipped privet. I breathe deeply. Across the night there is the heavy whispering of aircraft.

Way over the estuary, just discernable, are restless clusters of searchlights. The firefly stabbing of distant shell bursts. The grumbling of guns… increasing. Loud uneven throbbing now; heavy aircraft approaching rapidly.

The throb becomes a roar, filling the heavens. I am awestruck. Now the flares, row after row – I've never seen so many. Very pretty.

Still more. The swaying chandelier-flares descend casting mobile shadows, illuminating the city in a milky-white light. It's almost as daylight.

A lull in the gunfire. For moments the silence protrudes beyond the roar of aircraft. I can hear the popping of the parachute-flares opening up. Now the local guns open fire, at first sporadically. As the flares fade a new glow bathes the city and skies, quickly spreading and intensifying; this time the dazzling white from thousands of incendiary bombs rises from ground to heavens.

Transfixed, I watch the white glow turning orange and red. This time it's all happened so fast, so massively.

Dad comes up.

'What's going on son?'

'Just look at it,' is all I can gulp.

A hiss of bombs and I duck inside. Dad remains on the doorstep, but it's only incendiary bombs over OUR streets now. A few hundred incendiaries close by can sound like two or three big bombs.

There are warning whistles and the avenue fills with smoke. Men get to work with stirrup pumps, sand, even dustbins plonked on the things. Dad helps.

All hell is breaking loose. We take questionable cover at the street end of our back passage and gape, stunned.

A fantasia and compelling nightmare.

Over town and docks the red glow deepens, pulsates and periodically erupts in orange showers.

Above the glow searchlights playing on darker skies show up high-flying balloons and the smoke trails of snarling unseen aircraft as they make their shallow dive-bombing runs. Lately the bombers themselves have seemed harder to illuminate. Vicious shell bursts stab and crack; gun mizzle flashes, bomb flashes, huge flashes from the deadly land mines exploding after their sinister rustling descent by parachute.

A terrible beauty encompasses the city, mirrored on fiery skies.

After a while I dodge into a shelter with the others. Dad prefers the passage. The shelter gives a heave. Tentatively we look outside, but it's only windows gone, curtains streaming in the breeze, a downfall of soot. We are lucky.

Next day I pick my way to work in the town centre. A devastating journey, but the centre's worse. Still, our little office is safe and intact. The bosses live away from Hull.

My office colleague, though (there's just the cosy two of us) lives in Bean Street. Her house is flattened. She's safe in a shelter but evacuated and I am never to see her again although we write. Thank God she's not hurt. She's only 14 and so am I.

Nobody about. I leave the office early after tearing a page off the calendar – Thursday 8 May 1941. Fires still rage.

Nightfall. In clear skies there is a waxing half moon.

Over the town a dull ruddy glow, turned down but not out.

Occasionally the moon is disfigured as it sails through a rising haze. We wait.

They come again, simply stoke up the fires and repeat the performance. The second night is as bad if not worse. Bomb screams fill the mind and there are other screams – snarling engines and dive bombing to drop the parachute landmines effectively. A fantasia of smoke trails in the searchlights, the shattering anti-aircraft gun cacophony; the deadly rain of shrapnel clattering on tiles. Hull is burning, but not beaten.

A NIGHT OF TERROR

None of those who lived through it can ever forget the hell that was Hull in May 1941, the month of the big Blitz.

The city burned, and ordinary people fought a battle for survival.

Thousands were homeless, thousands more needed food and supplies.

This dramatic account vividly recalls the terrible aftermath of the bombing of 7 May.

It is late afternoon on 9 May 1941. You stand in the centre of a wrecked city. Last night the bombers came and brought horror and havoc in their wake. Today began the fight-back.

Firemen have been in action throughout the daylight hours. Rescue squads have been out picking through the rubble, listening for signs of life from beneath tons of masonry. Hospital staff have worked to the point of exhaustion tending the injured.

Across the city engineers have been out to asses the damage, followed in many cases by demolition gangs needed to clear damaged buildings which posed a danger.

Many large buildings in the city centre have been destroyed. Among those which, although damaged, survived the raid were the Guildhall and the Royal Infirmary. Almshouses, shops, offices, hotels, theatres and houses have suffered severely.

There were two hits on the Guildhall, one bomb crashing through the roof and exploding directly in front of the main entrance to the Council Chamber. Although certain parts of the building in this area were severely damaged, the chamber itself escaped serious harm and is expected to be in use next week.

The second bomb crashed through the roof and side wall of the banqueting chamber in which memorable and historic meetings have been held in years past.

In rooms of one floor of the Guildhall, not far from where the first bomb fell, members of the Women's Voluntary Services were on duty. Although the experience was terrifying, the women continued with their duties with magnificent calm and courage.

Damage to the Royal Infirmary, which had been struck on an earlier raid, is considerable.

It has been caused mainly by fire bombs which penetrated the building. It was evident early on that the raids were likely to be of great intensity and steps were quickly taken to remove patients from the wards on the upper floors to the greater safety of those on the bottom floor.

Luckily, the building escaped direct hits by high-explosive bombs, although buildings all around were demolished by this means. The terrific explosions of these bombs and the blast they caused shattered the Infirmary's windows and rushed down the corridors. Incendiaries in large numbers fell on the building and created fires at many points.

Staff have worked heroically and quickly managed to extinguish all the outbreaks.

They used stirrup pumps, sand and chemical extinguishers to help keep the flames in check, but as there were fears that the fire might spread along a ward all inflammable articles of furniture were thrown out of the windows.

Even then there was the danger that the burning embers from other fires in the neighbourhood might be blown through the smashed windows and this danger was counteracted by the removal of furniture into central corridors.

Realising the implication of what might happen, it was decided to evacuate all patients to the Sutton Annexe of the Infirmary.

Mr Bernard Sylvester, the assistant house governor who was in charge of the Infirmary at the time said it was the first time in 158 years that the hospital had been without patients.

He said:

'The bedraggled appearance of the staff after fighting the fires was some indication of the work they had done.

'They were covered with dust and grime with wet towels covering their faces to save their eyes from the blinding smoke and choking fumes.

'When dawn came it seemed miraculous that no one had received injury other than a few minor cuts and scratches.

'During a lull in the raid the nursing staff gave food and drink to all the patients. I am at a loss to understand how they managed this.'

The staff were on duty again during a subsequent night to attend to any air raid casualties who might be brought in. Although bombs rained down all around the building, it again escaped a direct hit, but it suffered further damage from the blast of the high-explosive bombs.

By good fortune, the Children's Hospital in Park Street has escaped serious damage.

Adjoining the hospital was a church schoolroom which was set alight and completely burned out, but due to the fire fighting by the staff the hospital was saved from damage.

There was great danger from an incendiary bomb which had lodged high on the roof, but a 16-year-old boy courageously ascended to the false roof, smashed his way through the tiles and at great personal risk climbed through and managed to dislodge the blazing bomb and knock it into the grounds below.

TWELVE
Fake gun 'protected' Hull

For the German raiders it was supposed to be a warning that Hull was ready to defend itself against the zeppelins that cruised high overhead.

On the ground it remained a carefully guarded secret but when the truth finally came out it attracted international attention, details of it even being featured in an American newspaper, the *Chicago Herald*.

The paper carried a story saying that the British government had succeeded in playing a joke on the people of Hull, claiming that they had gazed upwards to the roof of a local factory to watch soldiers go through the motions of preparing a gun for action, although never a single shot was fired.

The old and the new. The fake gun from World War One was placed on this factory. Rose, Downs and Thompson was to become Simon Rosedowns Ltd, and when this picture was taken in the 1970s the old part of the site was designated a listed building.

And the paper claimed that when a zeppelin arrived to drop its bombs it suddenly turned and sailed away without a single one hitting the ground.

Certainly the story most probably stretched things. But of one key fact there is no doubt whatever – there was a gun on the roof of a building known as The Forge, which stood at the corner of Cannon Street and Caroline Street. And it never did fire a shot, the reason being that it was made of wood.

The factory on which it stood was later that of Rose, Downs and Thompson and the imitation gun occupied a flat roof of a reinforced concrete building at the factory, having been installed on or about 5 July 1915 following the first zeppelin raid on the city and remaining there until it was removed on 23 January the following year.

In the intervening period there were numerous alarms that the Germans were approaching but no bombs were dropped.

The idea of installing a gun was initially put to the firm's managing director, Mr Charles Downs, but he was not told that it would be a dummy.

According to the one-time *Hull Times* journalist Arthur Tidman, who wrote of the gun in later years, it arrived at the Old Foundry during the midday meal hour when no workmen were around, but it so happened that the soldiers who brought it were seen lifting it onto the roof by a yard foreman who knew a thing or two about moving heavy machinery and soon realised from the way it was being handled that it could not possibly be real.

But up it went and official instructions were issued to the 'gunners' on duty that they would be on the roof from 8pm until 5am, remaining near the gun and ready to fire at a given signal.

According to Tidman: 'The man not on night duty was ordered to make, on arrival, some show of cleaning the weapon after which he was to replace the cover and report that "all is well".'

The order was signed by 'The Adjutant, RA Humber Defences.'

In 1934 more information came to light in a letter written by Major General J.A. Ferrier, who was in command of the Humber Defences, in

The aim of the fake gun was to warn off Zeppelin raiders who caused considerable damage in Hull during World War One. This picture shows the scene in Market Place after one raid. The photograph was issued as a postcard.

which he said that his original idea was to use rocket bombs to make a noise in the vicinity of the dummy gun when other guns opened fire.

So good was all this subterfuge that it was claimed the Germans were deceived and regarded the gun as a secret weapon to which it was wise to give a very wide berth.

It later transpired that the gun was removed following Mr Downs' continuing concern about its presence. He believed there could have been serious consequences if the deception became generally known among local people who had great confidence in the gun.

Concern, too, came from Sir Alfred Gelder, the MP for North Lincolnshire, who became so incensed at the authorities and their attempt to fool the public with a dummy gun that he raised the matter in the House of Commons.

At the time – it was still wartime – there was criticism of this, with some fearing his exposure would give valuable information to the enemy about the defencelessness of Hull, but Gelder argued that the Germans would know this anyway as they had met with no opposition when they raided the city in March 1916.

And so the saga of the dummy gun faded into history, well not quite for there was another, albeit light-hearted end to the story.

It came when someone, having noted Sir Alfred's Commons statement, submitted a mock tender for guns which the mystery writer hoped would conform to the requirements of 'The New Wooden Gun Department at the War Office'.

Tidman told us that the tender offered to supply one gun made of 'best deal painted two coats at 7s 6d' and another, tin-plated if required, which was guaranteed to 'take in the public all the time'.

'This second gun was priced at 25 shillings inclusive of a good hand barrow for touring gun posts.'

And what became of the gun?

It was simply said to have 'been disposed of'.

THIRTEEN
Royal scandal shocked the nation

Today the Hull Collegiate School carries the proud slogan 'Bringing out the best in everyone.'

But Tranby Croft, the fine building in which it is housed and which displays the mark of sophistication and elegance from a bygone age, a mansion once magnificent in its 34 acres of superb grounds, also carries the secret of what really went on over 120 years ago when Tranby Croft bore witness to an incident that certainly did not bring out the best in everyone.

At that time the home of Arthur Wilson, a businessman who played a major role in Hull's developing shipping trade, the house had 60 rooms, all richly decorated and furnished.

Wilson and his family moved into Tranby Croft in 1876. He was a man of taste and of standing in the community, a business leader who lived up completely to his family's motto – 'Business first and everything else afterwards.'

Like her husband Mary Wilson enjoyed the respect and admiration of her peers. She was a superb hostess, watchful of every detail, a socialite of standing and of style.

Both qualities were reflected in the company she kept, which included the Prince of Wales (later King Edward VII who was among the guests at Tranby Croft in 1890, a visit which should have been the supreme moment of the Wilson's social lives.

But as things turned out it helped link the family with a scandal that will be forever recalled whenever the name of Tranby Croft is mentioned.

Stately home. This was how Tranby Croft looked when pictured on a postcard in 1920.

Christopher Sykes was a snob. He just loved to be part of the high life and his determination to be a member of the circle which surrounded the Prince of Wales underlined that fact.

Regular dinner parties at not inconsiderable expense helped cement the relationship, and the events become quite famous. But such occasions led to Christopher, the MP for the Division of Buckrose in the East Riding, whose home was at Brantinghamthorpe, being ridiculed by many of those who knew him, his obsequiousness when in the presence of the royal guest being embarrassingly farcical.

Renton Heathcote in his book *Anlaby The History of an East Yorkshire Village* wrote: 'His servile response was typically "as your Royal Highness pleases" when in one of his more boorish moods the prince emptied a glass of brandy over his head and became a catchphrase with the Marlborough House set.'

But Sykes appeared to have been unperturbed by such put-downs and continued his lavish entertaining of the prince, spending so much money in fact that he ruined himself.

So the prince had to look elsewhere for a place to stay during race week – and that led him to Tranby Croft and one of the most famous trials ever heard in an English courtroom.

For the Wilsons the prospect of entertaining the Prince of Wales meant that they had truly 'arrived'. This was something extra special.

To make the occasion more memorable it was decided that as well as the prince his friends should be invited, too.

So, on 9 September 1890, the visit began with the prince and Sir William Gordon-Cumming, a long-time friend, arriving at Hessle by train, the station having been transformed for the event.

The scene was described by Gertrude M. Attwood in her book *The Wilsons of Tranby Croft*: 'The prince stepped down onto the scarlet carpet, which ran the full length of the platform (just to be on the safe side) and was met here by Arthur Wilson, his host, who also greeted the equerry, the Hon Tyrwhitt Wilson and Christopher Sykes, who should have been the host, not the guest.'

Dinner at Tranby Croft was a lavish affair, probably consisting of as many as 14 courses. The guests sat around a table which could seat eight people.

The meal over, entertainment was provided by Ethel Lycett Green who was well known as a singer and pianist.

But the prince wanted a little more excitement – and it was he who suggested that perhaps a game of baccarat might provide just that.

The game was, however, banned at Tranby Croft by Arthur Wilson, the reason being his son – Arthur Stanley, always known to the family as Jack – and his friends had been caught playing the game for high stakes on a previous occasion. His father stopped them and ordered the table removed and the counters to be confiscated.

Arthur realised that if he were to allow the game with the prince to go ahead his previous orders would appear meaningless. It is believed that with this in mind he left the room.

So the game went ahead, the prince playing with his own special counters made of Russian leather and carrying his feathers emblem. But as play progressed there were suspicions by some in the party that one of the players, Sir William Gordon-Cumming, was cheating by pushing forward extra counters to add to a placed bet when the cards

were falling in his favour and by increasing his stake by dropping counters from one hand over a single exposed counter, using the other hand to hide what he was doing.

After the game Mary Wilson was told and, aware that a scandal had to be avoided at whatever cost, ordered her son Jack, who had first become aware of what was happening, to keep his mouth shut.

Sir William Gordon-Cumming, the man at the centre of the Tranby Croft scandal, was said to be a notorious womaniser.

On the second night, Tuesday 9 September 1890, there were again suspicions that Sir William had cheated. He was well known in society circles, aged 42 and said by one paper to be 'possibly the handsomest man in London and possibly the rudest.' A Lieutenant Colonel of the 1st Battalion, Scots Guards, he was wealthy, owning 40,000 acres of land in Scotland.

On that second night there was additional drama. Mary's brother, Henry, died suddenly at his home in Crown Terrace on Anlaby Road. The family went into mourning.

Sir William Gordon-Cumming looked in the mirror to check that every detail of his dress was smart and correct.

A knock on the door brought him face-to-face with two senior members of the prince's party, neither of whom had been present during the baccarat sessions. They told him of the suspicions that he had cheated and that the prince would have to be informed.

Gordon-Cumming was stunned and angry. He had not, NOT, he repeated, been cheating. The very thought of it was an insult. He was a man of honour and integrity.

He demanded to see the prince himself and took the opportunity to again vehemently deny any misbehaviour.

But during the meeting a statement was produced which, it was suggested, he should sign with the aim of halting any leak of the allegations to the outside world.

It read:

'In consideration of the promise, made by the gentlemen whose names are subscribed, to preserve silence with reference to an accusation which has been made in regard to my conduct at baccarat on the nights of Monday and Tuesday 8 and 9 September 1890, at Tranby Croft, I will on my part solemnly undertake never to play cards again as long as I live.'

It presented him with a dilemma. Were he to sign it he would not know the names of those who would also sign it – so how many would be bound by it?

And if he did sign it then it would in effect brand him a cheat by his own admission.

His mind raced. Supposing he refused? Then the word would certainly get out about the scandal and he would be ruined anyway.

He signed.

But whether he was guilty or not Gordon-Cumming was to be branded for all time as the man who cheated.

Inevitably the story was to get out, despite attempts to keep the scandal quiet, and when this happened Gordon-Cumming decided that in order to try to protect what little honour he had left, to sue for slander.

The ensuing court case created a national outcry, the prince himself gave evidence. In the end Gordon-Cumming lost his case.

After the court case Gordon-Cumming retired to his estate in Scotland a ruined man.

High society never had anything to do with him again.

Arthur Wilson died at his home at Tranby Croft on 21 October 1909. He was 72 years old.

FOURTEEN
Stars of stage and screen

As always the room was grubby and noisy, the air thick with tobacco smoke and chatter.

Telephones shrilled and typewriters clacked incessantly as the day wore on.

Seated at the black Underwood typewriter, with its large keys and bell which rang as each line end was reached, Dorothy Mackaill reflected on her young life and, as she mechanically typed manuscript after manuscript, dreamed of a very different kind of work.

Dorothy, who was born on 4 March 1903, was just an ordinary girl from an ordinary house in an ordinary street in Hull when she began work at the *Hull Daily Mail*'s headquarters in Whitefriargate.

Always good-looking, she was a friendly, bright girl who had studied at Thoresby Street School. Her father John was manager of the Maypole Dairy on Spring Bank, which guaranteed the family a reasonable standard of living at a time when many faced considerable financial hardship.

John was also something of a local personality. In the evenings he took on his second job – that of master of ceremonies at the Newington Dance Hall.

After separation from his wife he moved from the family home at 15 Newstead Street to Anlaby, becoming postmaster and village confectioner, working in a shop on Hull Road. It did not prove a successful venture, however, and his stay in the village was short-lived.

Dorothy knew the only way to carve out the career she wanted was to move away from Hull. As the bright lights of showbusiness beckoned she took a decision which was to change her life dramatically, handing in her notice and heading to London to become a chorus girl at the London Hippodrome, appearing in a show called Joy Bells, which starred George Robey.

Star of the silver screen. Dorothy Mackaill, the Hull girl who became the world's highest-paid actress.

But London was one thing. America was another and it was the USA that attracted star-struck Dorothy. She moved to New York and landed a job on Broadway with the famous Ziegfeld Follies.

It was an event which would change her life.

Among the audience at the Follies one night was a director in the fast-expanding film industry. When he saw Dorothy he was impressed. She was good-looking, bright, bubbly and above all she had a real talent. He signed her up.

Dorothy made her first movie – *The Lotus Eater* – with John Barrymore in 1920. It was not long before she acquired the nickname that would remain with her for years to come – The Girl with the Bee-Stung Lips.

In the movie business the 1920s saw the end of the silent films, a development which was to lead to the end of their careers for some of the best-known names. Dorothy weathered this transition superbly and achieved stardom which was beyond her wildest dreams.

She signed a contract with First National Pictures which was worth £40,000 a year, a massive amount of money at that time, and was said to be the highest paid to any movie star at that point.

In the 1930s Dorothy Mackaill became a familiar name and a sought-after star, more often than not in the role later described as that of 'a vivacious flapper', an image reflected in some of the film titles, among them *Kept Husbands* and *Flirting Widows*.

In 1932 she starred in *Love Affair* with a new, up-and-coming leading man who would later become a silver screen legend – Humphrey Bogart.

But time caught up with her and her career faded in the mid-1930s. In 1937 she gave up the movie business, leaving to care for her ailing mother.

And for the next 50 years she lived in Honolulu, her only acting roles being small parts on the TV series *Hawaii Five-0*.

Dorothy Mackaill died of kidney failure in Honolulu, Hawaii in 1990 aged 87. She was cremated and her ashes were scattered at sea off of Waikiki Beach.

DUGGIE, A COMEDY PIONEER

When he took to the London stage they loved him, that son of Hull whose performances in the West End received wide acclaim. And then it was on to a career in movies with the offer of a Hollywood contract.

In a dazzling career he was hailed as a comedy pioneer, selected for the Royal Command performance and for a time headed a group of entertainers recognised as one of the funniest comedy teams in the country.

But despite his years of success Duggie Wakefield remains Hull's 'forgotten' star.

Duggie was not born in Hull, but moved to the city as a child and for ever after claimed Hull as his home town.

It was at Bridlington's People's Palace that an eight-year-old Douglas Wakefield made his first public appearance, singing *Thora* to lantern slides. The reason he used slides – to hide his face. He would later be described as 'long-necked, wide mouthed and goggle eyed'.

The Bridlington show lasted a week and for his performances he was paid five shillings. He said later he took this home in coppers so that it would look like a lot.

Those first appearances led to him being booked for a second week and then he went out with a juvenile revue as a boy soloist until his voice broke.

Of his early career Duggie wrote: 'At that time Charlie Chaplin was beginning to make his success and I was engaged by the same troupe to win his "Charlie Chaplin Competition" each week. The prize was ten shillings and a silver cup. I had to hand back the money to the boss as soon as I came off and the cup I had to keep clean.'

At seventeen and a half he went into the army where he proved successful as an entertainer, being made sergeant at 18 and running a concert party.

Duggie Wakefield was acclaimed as one of the country's funniest men, appearing in revue, variety, pantomime and films.

On demob he tried to make a living as a light comedian, but was not too successful, and joined a revue instead.

It was a turning point. He was 'spotted' and given a principal comedian's part.

Duggie made his first West End appearance as an extra choir boy with Gracie Fields in The Show's The Thing at the Winter Garden Theatre. Then he went into the show The Four Boys From Manchester at the London Palladium, again with Gracie Fields.

During one show he found himself playing opposite Gracie's sister Edith. For the show he wrote the song *I Just Can't Figure It Out At All* which led to them not only playing sweethearts on stage, but also embarking on a real-life romance, marrying during the run of the show.

Duggie then turned to the movies, playing an important comedy part in the Gracie Fields film *This Week of Grace*, and it was after this that his manager encouraged the famous American film producer Hal Roach to see Duggie's work when he appeared in a London music hall.

As a result he and Billy Nelson, who was appearing with him, were given long Hollywood contracts which led to them playing in numerous films

Throughout his life Duggie retained his love of his adopted city of Hull, proving the fact in December 1941 when he came to the Tivoli Theatre with a week's performance to benefit the Mother Humber Air Raid Distress Fund.

The *Hull Daily Mail* of the time reported the event and gave an insight to Duggie's real devotion to Hull and its people:

'For the Tivoli week Duggie is paying the salaries of the whole cast so that not only the normal theatre and printing expenses have to come from the takings. Duggie is forfeiting his own remuneration.'

It was not his first effort to help the fund. Earlier in the war he had paid a special visit to Hull to take part in a show and 'left an acceptable personal contribution'.

During his visits he stayed at 'a very pleasantly situated house' at Gilberdyke where his mother lived.

His success continued for several more years but on 14 April 1951 he died aged 51.

One report said of him: 'He can truly be said to have worked himself to death. For the last few years he had put more energy than he could spare into the knockabout comedy that had kept him working most of his life without a break in revue, variety, pantomime and films.

'Finally his doctor restricted him to an annual appearance in pantomime. His last show was *Cinderella* at Oxford. Only his closet friends knew that his bounding antics and horsey grin concealed the sufferings of a very sick man.'

HULL'S PAT WAS FIRST EUROVISION STAR

Her first public appearance was at a church festival at Derringham Bank Methodist Church in Hull where she was a Sunday School teacher.

It was a role that would lead her to a career which saw her star in West End productions, appear on Broadway as the leading female role in *Camelot* and in several major British feature films.

And there was more – her moment of true international fame came in 1957 when she was the first British star to sing at the Eurovision Song Contest.

Her name was Patricia Bredin. She was brought up at 182 Westlands Road, Hull and was a former pupil of Newland High School.

For a time she was a major star – and the first to recognise the fact was her singing teacher Miss Phyllis Hutchinson.

'I knew she was good,' Miss Hutchinson later told the *Hull Times*. 'I taught her to sing *The Voice of Spring* and after the festival people stopped to ask me if I had heard her.'

From there Patricia went on to join Hull Amateur Operatic Society – and then moved on to a career which would see her achieve national fame.

It was in 1957 that she made her first major breakthrough, being picked for Julian Slade's musical *Free As Air*. The *Hull Times* of April that year

Happy couple. Patricia Bredin is seen here with her husband, the singer Ivor Emmanuel. They married in 1964, but divorced within two years.

reported: 'To be linked with a Slade show is a sign of success for any girl on the way up, for he is one of the bright young men of British theatre.'

The show first aired in Leeds and at once Patricia – then 22 – was forecast for bigger things.

In London the show opened at the Savoy Theatre.

That same year came her appearance as the UK representative in the Eurovision Song Contest in which she sang a song called *All*, which was voted into seventh place. According to the official history of the contest the song, which lasted only one minute 52 seconds, is the shortest ever performance in the contest.

This really was the start of something big and a couple of years later Patricia Bredin was a star, by then appearing in feature films. In 1959 she made three movies. One – *Make Mine a Million* – starred Arthur Askey, then one of Britain's most popular comedians. In the second – *Desert Mice* – she sang. And in the third, which was called *Left Right and Centre*, she was given the leading female role opposite another well known Hull actor, Ian Carmichael.

April 1962 saw her take over for three months the role of Guinevere in the Broadway production of *Camelot* from Julie Andrews.

In 1958 the *Hull Times* reported that Patricia was married to Hull-born Stewart Murray who taught physical training and languages at Westminster School.

They met when she was 14 years old and were married in 1955 when Patricia was on tour and he had just graduated from Birmingham University.

The marriage was not to last and later the *Hull Times* was to report on her comfortable lifestyle with her second husband, the singer Ivor Emmanuel.

But the days of fame on stage and film were to be limited. By the early 1960s Patricia Bredin was becoming a name from the past.

There was still work, but in lesser musicals than those in which she had previously appeared.

According to one biographer: 'There seemed no reason why she didn't have more success. She looked intelligent and beautiful, and her singing made you sit up. Her film appearances (a luxury most of our unsung heroines have to do without) remind us of a highly attractive artist, one whom British musicals most unfairly and almost completely ignored.'

FIFTEEN
Shipwrecked hero's fight to live

They were men of courage who went to work in some of the most dangerous waters on earth, tough, hard men who fought nature at her worst. Yet still they returned to those hostile seas in search of adventure on voyages which over the years would claim the lives of thousands.

Some were men of education, officers usually, who recorded events they witnessed at first hand in diaries which present a vivid insight into their lives. This account is based on such writings and gives a chilling insight into the lives of men who crewed vessels from the port of Hull in the days of sail.

The agony was intense, the pain more than he could bear. He screamed again and again as the blade of the razor sawed into his foot. Then unconsciousness overwhelmed him and he sank into the darkness which relieved his pain until the task was completed. The operation, without anaesthetic, was the only way they could save him. But it didn't end with just one amputation, the second ankle, too, would be severed in exactly the same way.

And for months to follow he fought for his life, every day a struggle to remain sane as slowly his terrible wounds began to heal.

And finally they did.

Yet throughout all of this he retained a determination to survive, reflected in the message he scrawled on a piece of wood in the shape of a gravestone which marked the spot where his amputated feet were laid. It read:

Beneath this ground my feet do lay,

I've travelled on them many a day,

When safe at home oft shall I say,

'My feet lie in St George's Bay.'

They were the words of Anthony Ward, a rugged, God-fearing, sincere man who faced up to the worst that life could throw at him with amazing courage. And eventually this man of the sea was able to return home to Hull with a diary which recorded the dramatic events of a voyage that was to end in disaster and death for many others. This is his story.

They were almost ready to leave. On the deck Anthony Ward made his customary last checks, urging the crew to complete their tasks.

In the bright light of a summer morning the pilot had cheerfully announced his arrival at 7am, and three hours later the sailing ship *Columbus* inched her way from the Old Dock to be moored at Humber Dock gates.

Throughout the day workmen swarmed over the vessel, busy on last-minute preparations for her voyage. Finally ready she was hauled from the dock and to the transport buoy; the weather was now very different, with heavy rain lashing the estuary.

Finally, at 8pm, Commander George Orton let go the anchor in Hull Roads in seven fathoms of water, cleared the deck and set the watch.

The *Columbus* was ready for her voyage to Quebec. It was Monday 24 August 1835.

Wednesday 26 August. Wind south-east. Fresh breezes and dark, cloudy weather. At 8am got under weigh and turned down the Humber at 3pm, Brought up above Grimsby Roads. Strong winds and rain. Proceeded out of the Humber. Discharged the pilot, stowed the anchors. Set the watch.

Monday 23 November. After a long and tedious passage across the Atlantic Ocean with contrary winds and unpleasant weather, we arrived at Quebec in the latter part of October. Discharged our ballast and moored ship at Woolf's Cove and commenced taking on timber and deals…we completed our cargo about the 19th day of November.

And so *Columbus* sailed again, but it was not long before she ran into bad weather with strong winds and snow

Friday 27 November. The ship began to steer very badly, the rudder trunk being full of ice so we could only give the ship half her helm. In broaching *Columbus* shipped a most heavy sea in mid-ships which took the long boat from her chocks and laid her upon the lee rail. Also carried away all the lee bulwarks, likewise the deck lumber with chain cables washed most part overboard. Lost the topsail and the foresail boom broke. Ship making a deal of water, the pumps constantly going. The ship was like an iceberg and ourselves like detached pieces moving about her. The frost was so strong that the ropes of the ship were three times thicker than their usual size with ice.

Sunday 29 November. The ship nearly on her beam ends with water in her hold. At 11am saw three ships to the north westward. We then hoisted our signal of distress which was answered by the *Robert of Lancaster* who hauled his wind and stood towards us. The captain came on board and advised us to lose no time in getting our clothes and provisions and other necessaries out of the ship as night would draw in about four o'clock. The last boat left the ship with a pig, which we were obliged to kill before we put him in the boat as we were afraid he would capsize her. We left the *Columbus* with seven feet of water in her hold.

Saved, they now faced even more appalling weather conditions. So strong were the gales that the sails split and were swept away.

Tuesday 1 December. At midnight saw the land on the lee bow – an ugly coast. It was Newfoundland, mountainous black rugged rock. But we knew how we were situated and we found our only alternative was to run into St George's Bay at daylight

The ship was now fighting for her life and with little chance of success. Around her the wind howled and shrieked through the shrouds and mountainous seas battered her. The men on board had not a chance of saving her, knowing that the only hope was on the rock strewn coast on which she was destined to crash. Perhaps if they had known her – and their – fate, they would have preferred to die at sea.

Wednesday 2 December. When we got within Cape St George we had snow and sleet in masses and the weather was so deadly thick that we could not see the land. We conjectured that if we had a few days' fine weather we might get the sails and the ship put to right and so get a passage home. As the fog cleared away we saw the land and found we were on a lee shore and had not sufficient sail to beat the ship off, having a head wind and sea. Seeing no means of preventing the ship from going on shore we cut the anchors from the bows which brought the ship abreast of a rock nine feet above the sea upon which she struck with a tremendous crash. The sea passed over us with tremendous fury. We clung to the shrouds of the main mast, almost frozen to death and with the horrors of death menacing us from above and below. The sea was covered with the shattered bottom of the ship and the deals of the cargo. The *Robert* swung off and in for some time, but with the tide ebbing fast she turned on her broadside to the rocks by which we made our escape from her…there was nothing but death before our eyes. We all reached the beach except the captain of the *Robert* (Captain Gardner) and a boy who sank to rise no more. In leaving the wreck a heavy sea swept me from the rock and in the surf I lost my way, but providentially I found the beach after a desperate life and death struggle. On landing I found I had lost my shoes on swimming to the shore.

Thursday 3 December. We all walked along a rocky beach where my feet were much cut by the hard rocks for I was nearly barefoot with the exception of a pair of stockings with the feet out, which was a very poor protection upon rocks in such severe country.

Exhausted, wet and cold, the survivors next faced the task of climbing a cliff caked in ice in order to escape the heavy seas which pounded the shore. When we got up two feet we would slip down one, many a time the rock being like glass. At last we reached the top, but being cast upon a shore we were unacquainted with and having no leader, we hardly knew which way to steer. After a little consideration we walked on towards the bottom of St George's Bay.

At about 8am four more of our crew lost their shoes, which were pulled off in the woods for our way was much obstructed with piles of fallen trees and the snow which was sometimes four or five feet deep.

The steward of the Robert, a young man, gave up. He could walk no further and his shipmates who were with him were obliged to leave him or perish with him. As they proceeded his cries pierced their hearts till lost on the whistling breeze.

At noon, seeing no appearance of habitation to rest our weary limbs and nothing but thick woods as far as we could see from the top of the cliffs, we sat down upon the snow in despair.

We tried to get a light for a fire but everything was wet about us and our efforts proved all in vain.

As my feet were so badly cut by the rocks, they bled as I walked on the snow; the frost soon destroyed them of animal feeling. I cut up part of my pea jacket to cover them and then was obliged to take the neck handkerchief off my neck to tie the cloth on with as none of my shipmates had so much as a piece of yarn or twine about them.

We tried to make a place of shelter with the branches of fir trees but without success.

In the night feeble limbs carried us to the spot where the steward of the *Robert* was left. We found him lifeless, laid stretched on his bed of snow. The scene was heart rending in the extreme as we knew not how soon we should have to share his fate.

Friday 4 December. About 2am we reached the wreck, nearly exhausted with tired limbs, hunger and cold. Having no place of shelter and being unable to procure a light for a fire we remained on snow until daylight suffering the keenest pangs of hunger and cold owing to our scanty clothing in the penetrating frost.

At low water they again searched the beach for something to eat but all in vain. They all, except myself, again started in search of inhabitants.

Emaciated with hardships and unable to walk and also in a state of insanity they made me a place upon the snow and with branches of trees and laid me on it. They gave me a few wild berries to eat and took their leave one by one never more expecting to see me in the flesh. They were obliged to leave me to find inhabitants or die.

But there was hope. The exhausted men staggered onwards, at last finding two houses and food. As they ate, the owner, John Huelin, arrived. At last it seemed there was hope, but no one could have predicted the horror that was yet to come. Ward's diary became less detailed on a day-to-day basis, but his writings would still provide a graphic insight into the fate of the survivors:

I was quite insane. All the toes were cut off both my feet and the flesh cut off the soles of my feet.

Bluestones and poultices were applied to my wounds. I was in great pain and burnt up with fever and mortification was spreading fast.

I was obliged to have both feet cut off at the ankle joints with a razor by Thomas Legg on the 28th day of December 1835.

For two months my suffering was great as mortification had got up into the calves of my legs so that I could rest neither night nor day. At the same time the lower parts of them were like a piece of raw beef. All this caused excruciating pain. When the calves of my legs burst I was then relieved and after losing all my hair and getting a new skin I began to recover gradually to the great surprise of all about me for they never thought I would survive.

There was, however, more still to come as Ward fought against the ravages of frostbite with only the most primitive methods of medical surgery. He would write that in March 1836 the skin had healed down to his ankle bones, but the wounds were black with frostbite and the leg would not heal. His diary recorded:

I took them (the ankle bones) all four out with a penknife.

Six or seven other men lost their toes and seven more the greater part of them.

On Monday 23 May they finally left the area in a schooner belonging to the Heulin family. They were bound for Nova Scotia and arrived at Halifax a week later, eventually sailing for England on 12 June in the Royal Navy brig *Plover*, arriving at Falmouth on 4 July.

Ward was then taken to the London Hospital in Whitechapel for three and a half months, during which time he acquired a pair of artificial legs which cost him £10. Later he would continue his story in his diary…

I arrived in Hull on 19 November and from then until July 1838 I tried to get my wounds healed but without success so I consented to have my legs amputated higher up. The right leg was done on 3 July and the left one was done on 1 September by Dr Fielding.

It worked and Ward was able to get around on his cork legs, taking up the art of French polishing, at which he became proficient enough to gain employment.

But Hull was about to suffer tragedy: Cholera struck in 1845–46 and he was among its victims, dying within a few hours of the disease taking hold of him.

SIXTEEN

'Ordinary' man was notorious killer

Collier Street, Hull was typical of scores of other similar roads. Small houses built in rows and terraces offered few comforts and sanitary arrangements were primitive to say the least. Overcrowding was common and homes were dank, dark and dismal places.

No. 27 was probably no different to any other similar house in the 1860s and 1870s. Domestic surroundings there were as simple as they were inexpensive. Gas was almost unattainable by the poor and in thousands of households across the growing city of Hull the farthing rush light or the common tallow candle provided the only illumination – just enough to make darkness visible and nothing more. Here lived Charles Peace and his wife, Hannah, an ordinary couple, it seemed, keen to try to make a living, amiable when spoken too. At the time, though no one could have guessed their real story.

CHARLES'S STORY

My exploits are legendary. Even 130 years after they hanged me in Armley Jail for the murder of Arthur Dyson, of Sheffield, my reputation lives on. I also shot a policeman – PC Cock to be precise – and got away that one. Pity poor William Habron, who was sentenced to death for the crime he never committed, although he was, thanks to my confession made just before they hanged me, later released.

So that's me, Charles Peace, criminal. In middle age I was hardly the best looking of men, standing only 5ft 4ins tall, lacking fingers on my left hand, walking with my legs apart and speaking as if my tongue was too big for my mouth. I may not have been handsome, but it didn't stop me. Hannah, who became my loving wife for a time, never minded, anyway.

I got by in crime largely because of my nerve, I suppose. I was also a master of disguise, one of my favourites being that of a one-armed sailor. I made a hollow dummy arm through which I put my real arm to hide my maimed left hand. At the end of this was a hook which proved useful on countless occasions when I was climbing the outside of a house while on the rob.

I remember well one time when I shaved my beard, dyed my skin dark and passed for a half caste.

But I was always respectably dressed because I knew the police would never think of suspecting anyone who appeared in good clothes. Now the coppers were easy to fool, and I should know for I did just that, time after time.

I always believed that a policeman goes by the face and never thinks of looking at a man's hands.

Now you may wonder what an ugly looking bloke like me was doing with a wife. Surely women would not be attracted by me, you might think. But Hannah, bless her, was. And we had a couple of kids together, too, although I was never to see my son for he was born while I was in prison.

Anyway, my story in Hull goes something like this. We moved to 27 Collier Street, near the bus station, and set up a business. Writers have variously described it as an eating house or a provision shop and I suppose it was probably a bit of both. Anyway it served its purpose as a hide for me and helped me successfully cover my tracks.

Crime, I suppose, was my only real way of getting by. Born in Sheffield, I had an accident in childhood which left me something of a cripple. This meant I was unable to attend school as much as I should have and throughout my life I was barely able to read or write.

Work was irregular, although I did give it a try. Look through my police records and you'll find I was a joiner, carver and gilder at one time. But basically I was lazy. There were easier ways of making a living.

It was a gold watch which started me in my criminal career and to begin with I was not terribly successful. In fact I received successive sentences of four, six and eight years penal servitude before coming into the limelight as the criminal of my generation, a title of which I remain proud.

One writer summed me up pretty well, I think, when he said: 'The exploits which led to his acquaintances with prison revealed him as a desperado – resourceful, violent and sticking at nothing when cornered.'

Anyway, enough of all that. You're probably wondering how I came to be in Hull and I'll try to explain.

I was serving my eight years in Wakefield and tried to escape but was caught in the act while I tried to cut a hole in the ceiling of my cell to gain access to the roof. When they found me I managed to knock down a warder and run into the governor's house where I nicked his clothes and hoped I could get out in disguise. Needless to say it didn't work.

The real highlight of my career, though, was when I sat in the court at Manchester during the trial of two brothers named Habron for the murder of PC Cock.

Then I committed another murder, shooting Albert Dyson, who was a civil engineer and whose wife had been responsible for a warrant being taken out for my arrest.

I decided to get out of Sheffield and I made my way back to Hull.

I reckoned I had got away with it, but a copper had been told to watch the house and despite my disguise called his mates. I got away, though – they never thought of looking for me on the roof, hidden behind a chimney stack.

Peace certainly had cheek. On one occasion in Hull he saw PC Pearson posting bills relating to burglaries in the town and offering a £100 reward.

Seeing that he was the wanted man and was described as having a long grey beard he shaved it off and moved to Nottingham.

There he became acquainted with Susan Gray and together they returned to Hull as Mr and Mrs Thompson. They took apartments at a house in Cambridge Street facing St Luke's Church. The house was kept by a Mrs Rothwell, wife of PC Rothwell.

Imagine me living in a copper's house! Well it happened in Hull and I enjoyed staying there for a couple of months. The trouble was that Susan discovered who I was, which didn't help for a time.

For a week we had accommodation in Paragon Street. Generally I was known as John Ward and was quite well known in town, working in the Humber Street fruit market. In the evenings I went to the pub, usually the Carlton (later the Albany Hotel) in Waterworks Street, although I didn't drink much at all.

During my time in Hull there were many burglaries, which were later attributed to me. Then I visited York, where similar crimes were reported.

The end really came when I was robbing at Blackheath and was surprised by PC Robinson. I shot him five times, tried to make my escape but was caught and got penal servitude for life. While under arrest I wrote a letter and dropped myself in it by referring to John Ward, which led them to interviewing me for the Dyson murder.

After one more desperate attempt to escape from a train, on which he managed to dive through the open window, Peace went to the gallows.

He died in Armley Jail in 1879.

His last words were 'God bless you all.'

SEVENTEEN
Hero of the business world

He was a man of wealth, a self-made millionaire from Hull who had one other ambition:

Joseph Rank did not want to die while still being an extremely wealthy man.

Nor did he. For when his will was published in 1943 he left £70,950 gross. Most of the rest he gave away to good and charitable causes.

Joseph came from a family whose activities in milling went back to the early decades of the 19th century, when John Rank entered the trade at Sproatley. Subsequently he moved to Hull.

One of John's four sons, James, set up on his own account in a small windmill in Southcoates Lane and later moved to a bigger mill at Stepney.

It was there that Joseph, another of James' sons, learned the rudiments of the trade. In later life he was to recall: 'There was no overtime then and we had to work as long as the wind blew to turn the sails. On Saturdays if there was no wind we were let off at six o'clock.'

But his brothers were slow movers and in 1875 Joseph launched out on his own, hiring Mr Waddingham's mill in Holderness Road, Hull for three days a week.

About this time huge quantities of super grade white flour were being imported from the United States, made by steel roller presses of English manufacture.

The anomalous state of affairs and the popularity of the American flour impressed Joseph, who determined to fight this competition.

Land was bought in Williamson Street, Hull and in 1885 his first roller mill, the Alexandra, was started, to be followed by the Clarence Mills on the banks of the River Hull.

Man of his time. J. Arthur (Lord) Rank really proved the point when he was chosen to appear on the front cover of the highly acclaimed Time *magazine.*

After Clarence Mills had been established Joseph Rank startled London by erecting great mills at the Victoria Docks to supply the London demand.

Subsequently he went further afield to Cardiff, Birkenhead and Ireland, entering into associations with firms in Edinburgh, Glasgow and Selby.

Ultimately, for nearly £2 million in cash, he secured control of Associated London Flour Millers and in 1933 Ranks Ltd was floated as a public company with a capital of £7,295,000.

Straight and honest in all his dealings, energetic and industrious, far-sighted and enterprising – these were the qualities of Joseph Rank.

Yet he had very little formal education beyond the three Rs.

Possessed of the Yorkshireman's love of money, Joseph Rank found pleasure in making it and even greater enjoyment in giving it away.

Though a man of great riches he was nevertheless careful in money matters and his mode of life. He was a teetotaller and non-smoker.

It is said that during his lifetime he gave more than £2 million to Methodism and to Hull he gave upwards of £300,000 to form the nucleus of the Joseph Rank Benevolent Fund.

He had no taste for politics, nor did he covet public honours. When asked to allow his name to be put forward for inclusion in a Birthday Honours List his reply was: 'What would I do with a title. I'm Joe Rank to everybody, they wouldn't recognise me as Sir Joseph.'

But one honour he was delighted to accept was that of having his name added to the list of Hull's illustrious honorary freemen.

EIGHTEEN
The legacy of Thomas Ferens

A boss says 'be there on time'. A leader is there ahead of anyone else. This, in a nutshell, describes the Rt Hon T.H. Ferens, punctuality being one of the maxims of his life.

Thomas Robinson Ferens was born at Shildon, County Durham on 14 May 1847, the second son of George Waller Ferens and Anne Jackson, Educated privately at Bishop Auckland he entered the Shildon office of the Darlington and Stockton Railway at the age of 13.

In 1868 he came to Hull – a city of which in later years he was extremely proud – as shorthand and confidential clerk to Mr (later Sir) James Reckitt.

He was at the time well practised in shorthand as it was his habit to take down the sermons in church twice every Sunday.

In 1868 there were in Reckitts about six clerks and between 200 and 300 people. When Mr Ferens died in 1930 he was chairman of the company of Reckitt and Sons.

In 1873 Mr Ferens married Miss Esther Ellen Field, daughter of Mr William Field, of Hull, who he had met in the course of his church work. Mrs Ferens died in 1922. There were no children of the marriage.

T.R. Ferens was Liberal MP for East Hull from 1906 to 1918 and, in 1912, was honoured by King George V by being made a member of the Privy Council. The same year he was made High Steward of Hull, having already received the Freedom of the City.

He was more than once offered a title, but this he refused as he felt that he would always rather be known as plain 'Mr'.

From the time Mr Ferens first earned a salary he always put aside one 10th of his income to give to charity and in later years he gave more than that, his benefactions were well known.

The Ferens Art Gallery and a donation of £250,000 to found the University College of Hull were perhaps the most publicised of his gifts.

Education was dear to his heart and various schools and colleges had reason to be thankful for his munificence.

Years after Mr Ferens' death Ferensway was named after him.

When he died he left his home – Holderness House – to be used as a home for gentlewomen in reduced circumstances.

It is said that T.R. Ferens never forgot a face and his interest in the children of East Hull and their families never waned.

He was also very fond of animals and one diary entry reads: 'Tim (trap horse) died today. Served without fault for 17 years. Big hearted, efficient old boy.'

NINETEEN
Robbed by his own employees

They said his bark was worse than his bite. But no one who knew him would want to cross swords with Martin Samuelson, a man once described as 'a terror in debate, a little too hasty to take offence, perhaps momentarily too resentful of unpalatable criticism'.

No one, though, could take away from him his success as a ship builder.

Martin Samuelson began business in Hull in 1849 as a marine and general engineer, millwright and iron and brass founder.

Five years later his premises were extended and the firm entered the iron ship building business, soon operating from a yard situated at the mouth of the Old Harbour on land which was reclaimed at great expense in 1858 and which eventually covered an impressive 12 acres.

In his *History of the Town and Port of Kingston-upon-Hull* (1866) James Sheahan says:

'On the premises is a patent-slip considered one of the best in use which is worked by hydraulics. This is capable of taking ships of the very largest burthen for repairs. Indeed, for complete appliances and extent of building ground there are few, if any, establishments in the United Kingdom to be compared with, and better adapted, for ship building purposes than this.'

Samuelson's yard was a massive success, not to mention a major Hull employer. In just 10 years a total of 95 vessels, most of them steamers, were built there.

Sheahan reported: 'In March 1864 there were 14 vessels on the stocks in the yard. These have varied from 300 to 3000 tons burthen and from 100 to 1000 horse power. In 1863 the firm built a larger number of vessels than any other firm in the kingdom.'

It was a huge success story – on one occasion four ships were launched at the yard in one morning – but Samuelson the businessman was to fall victim to his workforce.

Henry Corlyon, a Hull journalist in the 19th century, takes up the story:

'In plain English he (Samuelson) was the victim of employees who, in many instances – and it could only have been with connivance – drew large sums which were never earned.

'This was at a time when men in our shipbuilding yards earned a pot of money.

'I was once told that the men on night shifts, to allay suspicion, would arrange with boys to keep up a constant hammering on the plates whilst they took it in turns to either snooze or booze until their shift ended. Clever people will ask "why was not the fraud detected?"

'I am not clever enough to answer that but there must have been a nefarious connivance. Certain it is that some men made far more out of the yard than did Mr Samuelson and I have often heard houses not built by the owner of the yard described as "Samuelson's Folly".

TWENTY
Hull's forgotten inventors

Few today will ever have heard of Thomas Todd.

He was born in Hull. He died in the town in 1849. And he worked as an engineer.

But he was also a man of foresight and ingenuity, a fact reflected in the items he produced.

In 1796 he invented and manufactured 'Todd's Original Copying Machine' which was later in use in both this country and abroad.

The following year he patented a 'new invented hydraulic pump for raising water and other liquids'.

Todd's achievements did not end there, though.

In 1832 he came up with a marine fire engine and in 1839 there came on the scene 'Todd and Firth's Improved Self Adjusting Paddles for Propelling Steam Vessels.'

Mr Todd was also said to have invented many other articles, among them a special type of kit for saving lives after shipwrecks. He was also the first person to introduce coal gas into the town.

James Wright was a confectioner who owned a shop in Osborne Street. He became well known as an artist who spent much of his leisure time on rustic modelling, chiefly in cork, which earned him an enviable reputation. One writer said of him: 'There is no exaggeration in asserting that for artistic conception and mechanical completeness, most, if not the whole, of Mr Wright's works in cork cannot be surpassed.'

But Wright had another claim to fame – locally at least.

For he was the manufacturer of what was known as Myton Toffy.

According to the 19th-century historian James Sheahan: 'When Prince Albert Victor passed through Hull in 1864 our confectioner-artist presented the future monarch of these realms with a box of his "toffy". A few weeks later an order for a quantity of this Hull "lollypop" arrived from the chief seat of English royalty, and Mr Wright afterwards received a missive dated "Windsor Castle, 27 March 1865" and signed "Fitzgerald", testifying that the Myton Toffy "is superior to any yet introduced into the Royal Household".

TWENTY-ONE
Furniture for the rich and famous

For the rich and famous seeking to furnish their mansions both in England and abroad there was just one place to go – Bond Street in Hull.

For it was there they would find the impressively large headquarters of Richardson and Sons, the largest furniture manufacturers in the country.

The business was founded in 1812 in Dagger Lane by Thomas Richardson, who was reputed to have been one of the finest cabinet makers of his day, and was later expanded by three of his sons.

The buildings the business occupied consisted of four blocks and extended from Bond Street into Waltham Street. The front cabinet showrooms measured 100 square feet and the two upper stories, which contained galleries, were lighted by a glass dome.

The goods produced received wide acclaim and were enthusiastically reported on.

One historian would write: 'Every article of first class furniture, suitable either for the church, the palace or the mansion, is designed and manufactured here from the rough log and carried out to the utmost finish and polish and it is a somewhat remarkable circumstance that mansions are furnished by the Messrs Richardson, not only in every part of this kingdom but in many parts of the European and American continents.'

Locally the impact of Richardson and Sons was seen in the Town Hall, built in 1862, which was largely furnished by them.

They also made a special set of chairs for use by Queen Victoria when she visited the city with Prince Albert in 1854.

TWENTY-TWO
King of the whalers

In the stillness of night the cry of a baby broke the silence that enveloped the surrounding streets, the small, shrill sound of a newborn carefully placed in the cot beside his mother's bed.

Proudly, the boy's father looked down on his son as the midwife busied herself making the room clean and tidy again, pausing to ensure that the resting mother was comfortable after the ordeal of giving birth.

For Robert Standidge this was the second time that he had become a father, his first son having been born to an earlier marriage. It was a situation which bothered him, one which would, in times to follow, see him upon his death leave the whole of his property, a substantial holding by all accounts, to that first child.

Of his newly born son he would simply say: 'Samuel had brains enough to work his own way.'

And that is exactly what happened.

Amid a mass of ships' masts and men Samuel Standidge looked down from the harbour side with pride as last minute preparations were made for a journey of adventure.

It was 1766 and at 39 years old he was living up well to his family's reputation as seafarers.

From his childhood he had yearned for a life on the oceans and had, as soon as he was able, entered the merchant marine to begin a career which saw him rise rapidly to officer level. Indeed, by the age of 19 he had been accepted as a young man who really was destined for higher things, being mate and later master of vessels making voyages to North America.

It was a lifestyle which saw him quickly appreciate the dangers inherent with seagoing life in that era.

This is No. 1 High Street, Hull, once owned by adventurer Sir Samuel Standidge. It was one of two properties of his and was used for his business affairs. His second property was his impressive home at Thorngumbald which was set in 200 acres of land.

That came about in 1744 when as mate of a ship he fell foul of the French, with whom Britain was at war, for while returning from Virginia to Hull with a cargo of tobacco, he was captured and taken to Cape Francois on the north coast of Hispaniola in the West Indies and later to Rhode Island.

Things looked grim for a time, but it was an imprisonment which would later stand him in good stead as he learned much about the locality in which he was held.

That came about in 1749 when Standidge was master of a vessel called *American*, which ran into a violent snowstorm while off Nantucket Island; Nantucket is 30 miles south of Cape Cod, Massachusetts...

Nantucket was a great interest to me and would play an important part in my early seagoing life.

While imprisoned by the French I learned much about that region and this was of great value to me when *American* ran into severe problems.

The snow was as bad as I have ever seen, whipped by gale-force winds and bringing visibility to nothing. We strove to keep our head to wind, the crew were exhausted as waves threatened to overcome us. Thankfully, the storm soon abated and I was able, largely through my knowledge of the area, to keep us on a course which took us away from the dangers the coastline held.

In the end we came through it, but that place would also hold a memory for me. For at the time it was the world's leading whaling port, an industry which had begun there as far back as 1672.

Standidge returned to Hull and, following his success as a ship's master, soon found himself entering the business on his own accord, buying and trading vessels of his own and then going one stage further and building them. The scene was set for his next venture – whaling…

The Dutch were the real masters of the whaling trade, which was first said to have been carried out from Rhode Island in 1598. Initially it was Hull merchantmen who exploited this great fishery but then they failed to capitalise on it, allowing their rivals from across the North Sea to do so. I was well aware of the rewards that whaling could bring and decided to enter the trade myself, equipping and sending a vessel to Greenland, which proved quite successful. In the following two years two more went out there, on one of which – the *British Queen* – I sailed as master.

So began my love affair with the northern regions, my appetite for exploration having been whetted by the Honourable Daines Barrington, who had planned an expedition but failed to see it leave following long delays.

I was determined to push ahead with my plans and had every intention of commanding my own vessel, but this was not to prove possible.

The problem was that in 1775, the year I had intended to sail, I was appointed Sheriff of Hull and while on the verge of boarding the ship was summoned by the Recorder of the town who informed me that because of my official position I was legally barred from leaving the kingdom. I was both angry and saddened, but such is the responsibility of the office of Sheriff I had but little choice.

Disappointed, but undeterred, Standidge continued to retain interest in whaling and by 1788 owned four ships out of the 35 which sailed from Hull to Greenland.

During this period he branched out into another business, that of seal skins, becoming the first man in Britain to have these tanned, the leather

Stately homes? Not exactly, but as this picture shows houses in High Street, Hull, just down the road from that owned by Sir Samuel Standidge were impressively grand.

being produced at Beverley and initially used to make shoes for himself and his family. Before this the bulk of the skins were simply thrown overboard. And there was yet more success on the horizon…

My next important venture came in 1789 when Russia and Turkey went to war. I was fully aware, as were others, that the Russians were in great need of transport ships and I had at that time within my fleet vessels which had been used for that purpose by our government. I decided to offer the Empress Catherine three of them on the same terms as I had received from the British Navy Board, the offer was quickly and gratefully accepted with a request for a further 50 similarly large ships for the same purpose, which I was able to obtain, and all sailed in April 1790 under Admiral Erf. Later I would receive not only thanks from the Russians for this but also the honour of an imperial decoration in the form of a Maltese cross in gold

Man of action. Sir Samuel Standidge.

and set with topazes conferred upon me by Emperor Paul.

In 1795 – the year he was knighted – Standidge became Mayor of Hull. He was also Master Warden of Trinity House on five occasions.

But despite the ceremonial and fulfilling role of a leading citizen he always hankered after adventure, a trait underlined by an incident in the Humber…

Like most others at the time I was interested to hear that an area which would become known as Sunk Island was recovered from the Humber. At first it was laid claim to by the Constable family, the Lords Seignory of Holderness, a decision which was opposed by the government and this led to a hearing at the assizes in York, at which I was called to give evidence.

I told the court of my own experience when, returning to Hull in one of my own vessels, I was chased by another ship, a privateer, and managed to avoid him by sailing through a passage known as Stone Creek between Sunk Island and the mainland. My evidence was sufficient to see the Constables lose claim to the land.

But time was beginning to take its toll and in 1798 Standidge's business was taken over by the firm of Halls, Ellison and Richardson.

Standidge died on 19 February 1801 at the age of 76. He is buried in the north aisle of St Mary's Church, Lowgate.

TWENTY-THREE
Hull's dark winter of 1968

It was a day Hull would never forget.

The men on the trawlers *Lorella* and *Roderigo* were lost without trace in appalling weather conditions off northern Iceland on 26 January 1955.

More than half a century later the last dramatic messages from the vessels still make chilling reading.

The time, early morning:

***Lorella* to *Roderigo*:** Boat deck solid with frozen snow. Lads digging it out since breakfast. Terrible lot on bridge top and they are going out there in daylight if possible.

***Roderigo*:** Same here and the whaleback is a solid mass.

14.21 *Roderigo*: One side of our aerial is down, weather very bad and freezing.

14.36 *Lorella*: Heeling over.

14.39 *Lorella*: Going down, heeling over. *Lorella* going down, heeling over. That was her last transmission.

15.53 *Roderigo*: Calling all ships, we are now taking heavy water.

16.30: Aerials now icing up.

16.45: Can anyone take a bearing on this frequency.

***Lancella*, which was in shelter and listening into the broadcasts:** Bearing as near as can say north-east.

16.50 *Roderigo* to Lancella: Come to us. Position becoming serious now.

16.52 *Lancella* to *Roderigo*: We are coming to you.

An American aircraft from the USAF base on Iceland now asked *Lancella* for

Roderigo's position. **Lancella replied:** *Roderigo* is 90 miles NE of Iceland's North Cape. Wind NE force 11–12, visibility nil to one cable.

Aircraft to *Roderigo*: What are your intentions?

17.04 *Roderigo*: No intentions. Going further over. No visibility. Still going over to starboard.

17.05: Still going over to starboard. Cannot get her back.

17.08: Still going over, going over.

17.09: *Roderigo* going over.

The message was repeated in Morse until, after three minutes, transmission ceased.

Two vessels lost. And 40 fishermen dead.

The tragedy highlighted one basic and undisputed fact – that distant water fishing was Britain's most hazardous business. Throughout the 1950s the death rate for British trawlermen was several times higher than that of coal miners. Many others suffered serious injuries including loss of limbs, and chest and breathing complaints from which they would never recover.

Their conditions were like those faced by men in no other industry.

In the darkness of Arctic winter they lived and worked in some of the worst weather on earth. In a 10-day period a man could be on duty for as long as 180 hours. And contrary to popular belief the rewards he received at the end of a trip could hardly be described as generous.

The trawlerman's lot was probably best summed up by the sociologist Jeremy Tunstall in his book *The Fishermen*, first published by MacGibben and Kay in 1962. He wrote: 'The fisherman believes his to be the harshest, the least well remunerated and the least understood job in Britain. Since the occupation, with few exceptions, attracts men who have failed to undergo apprenticeships and acquire skills, and since to start fishing in the first place the men must be willing to work what on shore would be fantastic hours under fantastic conditions, it is not unreasonable to say that all fishermen without exception have a common picture of their job. And since the job takes up three quarters not only of their days, but also of their nights and weekends and shapes the other quarter of their times ashore, fishermen tend to share a common picture of the world.'

Those who crewed the fishing vessels would know exactly what he meant. For, to a large extent, fishing was a job which enveloped whole families. Generations would follow each other to the northern fishing grounds. They knew the dangers and accepted them. It was all a part of their calling.

And dangerous it most certainly was. Between 1948 and 1964 a total of 757 British fishermen died as a result of accidents at sea. It was an occupation ably summed up by a skipper: 'We can live through the hurricanes. We ride them out, dodging to the wind. The spray freezes as it hits the rigging at an inch a minute, the masts get top heavy and the rails a solid wall. The funnel gets a six inch coating of ice. You try to clear it and back it comes. She rolls and pitches and you're scared. But it's the only job we know. Fear is just a part of it.'

The severe gales and icing conditions which seriously endangered trawlers at sea were accepted as relatively exceptional occurrences. But bad weather is found in Icelandic waters every winter and made the work of the individual fisherman on deck arduous as well as dangerous.

It was a situation summed up succinctly by the Admiralty Arctic Pilot: 'In the Denmark strait during December to April, inclusive, it is quite common for a north easterly gale to last several days with air temperatures below 29°F. North easterly gales preponderate over those from other directions on most of the Icelandic fishing grounds, particularly near the north western coasts, where they not uncommonly exceed Beaufort force 12. In these conditions very high seas are generated, wave heights reaching 50ft and more. Vessels steaming even slowly against such seas ship a lot of water and in sub-freezing temperatures ice may rapidly form great loads on the upperworks.'

Tunstall, a research officer at the London School of Economics, gave a graphic description of life on a trawler deck in an article for *New Society* magazine published in 1963. He wrote: 'In any sort of a wind spray flies into the men's faces and fishing is not stopped until the wind reaches nearly gale force. In winter the fish freeze stiff on the deck; the deckhand must bend down for each one, manipulating his gutting knife with cold hands. The hands of an old deckhand are swollen and marked by years of frost and cuts. All the time the deckman is on the deck there is the chance of a freak wave knocking him over into the fish and swirling him away across the deck. After only five hours of sleep the deckhand must turn out for more than 18 hours of this harsh routine. The only respite is provided by gale force winds when a trawler rolls and pitches crazily.'

After the disaster of 1955, and that which was to follow in 1968, measures were at last taken to attempt to cut down the dangers faced by trawlers on the traditional Icelandic fishing grounds. It was a move too late to save 98 men, but at least it was an acceptance of the dangers they faced in their everyday working lives.

Introduced the winter following the 1968 disaster, a 'mother ship' became a fixture on the Icelandic fishing grounds, providing an essential weather reporting, hospital and communications service.

But the days of the distant water fishing fleet were numbered. Cod wars led to permanent exclusion from the fishing grounds. The British distant water fleet, once the biggest and best in the world, was dismantled. The plight of the fishermen is now a part of social history. But it is a chapter which must never be forgotten.

St Andrew's Dock, Hull, March 2010

This is a place of memories.

From here men once sailed to some of the most dangerous waters in the world. They do so no more.

The trawlers in which they sailed have been committed to the scrapyards, converted to rig supply vessels, sold abroad…and forgotten.

The men who sailed them are now home from the seas for the rest of their lives. Many are without a finger, an arm or a leg, the results of accidents while working on open decks lashed by gales, blizzards and mountainous waves. Others suffer the effects of working over-long hours in some of the most hostile conditions on earth, victims of chest and lung conditions from which they will never recover.

And many more are lost for ever, their graves unmarked and unknown, victims of the cruel sea.

This dock was once the centre of Britain's, if not the world's, finest fishing industry.

Today the ships are gone, then men are gone and many of the buildings are long-vanished, too.

Distant water fishermen were for too long the poor relations of British industry. And when their industry finally collapsed they were cynically dumped by a system that held them in little regard. Not for them the generous pay-out to miners or steelworkers.

That, like St Andrew's Dock, is part of maritime and industrial history. But the stories of these men who worked together, lived together and all too often died together, must be recorded. They are a part of not only Hull's heritage, but also of the history of the British working man.

For the distant water fisherman the march of progress which split up his community after one hundred years in the Hessle Road area of Hull brought contact with other workers on the vast new estates built around the city. And, in turn, the knowledge of other ways of life and conditions of work brought the inevitable comparison with the fisherman's own lot.

The spotlight on trawlermen began to focus on their long hours of work under harsh conditions, on the incidence of casualties, on the lack of social security and proper vocational training, on occupational health hazards and the casual system of employment. But such concerns came too late. Economics and politics combined to annihilate the distant water industry. The fishermen were, yet again, the victims.

St Andrew's Dock made some men millionaires. It brought others only hardship and adversity.

Some still care to remember the deeds of men who sailed to some of the most dangerous waters on earth. Each year they gather at the lockhead on what remains of the Hull Fish Dock to pay tribute to the 5,000 fishermen who in little over a century sailed from this port never to return.

This is the story of 58 of them.

St Andrew's Dock, Hull, 10 January 1968

It was an uneventful parting.

With a single blast of her siren she slipped through the lockhead and into the Humber in a well rehearsed procedure practised and perfected by generations of fishermen.

In the early hours of a freezing winter morning few had turned out to see her leave. Goodbyes were said earlier, in the pubs, the clubs and the terraced houses that were home to so many of the men of the Hull trawler fleet.

A freshening northerly whipped up the swirling, muddy waters of the river as the trawler slid easily past the waterfront and down towards Spurn. In the city, frost glinted under the street lamps like a carpet of crystal as Hull slept.

Aboard the trawler 20 men shrugged off the memories of three days ashore and slowly eased themselves into the well-worn routine of making her ready for sea.

Deep below decks the engines that could carry her at a maximum of 12 knots purred steadily as she pushed on relentlessly, bound for the Norwegian fishing grounds.

She was called *St Romanus* and like others of her kind she was rugged, functional, yet strangely stylish, built to a design tried and tested in some of the world's most hazardous waters.

Eighteen years earlier she had left the Beverley yard of Cook, Welton and Gemmell to be handed over to the Belgian firm which commissioned her and originally called her the *Van Dyck*. She was now in the ownership of the Hull trawler company Thomas Hamling, who bought her in March 1964.

For this one trip *St Romanus*, which carried the number H223 on her side, was under the command of Skipper James Wheeldon, known to those who served under him as careful, prudent man. Normally in command of another Hamling vessel, *St Andronicus*, he had not particularly wanted the trip. Indeed, he did not have high regard for *St Romanus*.

The vessel he now commanded was just over 170ft in length, weighed 600 tons, and for this trip carried a crew of 20. It was not a full complement, for there was no radio operator aboard. Instead the skipper would handle communications.

By 7.30pm she was making good time and was, said Skipper Wheeldon in a radio telephone conversation with his wife, Janet, 120 miles north-north-east of the Humber. He had tried for two hours to make the radio work. During his call, reception fluctuated from good to almost indecipherable. The operator intervened and asked him to change frequencies. Above the crackle of static he promised he would call again the next morning. He never did.

As *St Romanus* was creeping steadily northwards towards Norway a second trawler was also heading out into the North Sea, but she was destined for Icelandic waters. In three weeks she could expect to sail well in excess of 2,000 miles.

She was the *Kingston Peridot* and she, too, came from the Beverley yard, having been built just 20 years earlier for the Kingston Steam Trawling Company. She measured 181ft in length, was over 657 tons in weight and could turn in a speed of 13 knots when pushed to the limit.

Like *St Romanus* she carried 20 men. One of them was a radio operator.

Slowly, steadily, she worked her way along a coastline by now hidden from view as night crept in.

It had been an unremarkable day.

ISAFJORDHUR, ICELAND, 11 JANUARY 1968

Thordur Oddsson was relaxed and satisfied.

As first mate of the Icelandic trawler *Vikingur 111* he had little to complain about. Catches had been good and the weather had proved kind. A few more hauls and it was back to port. Oddsson idly flipped through a magazine as he rested on the bridge.

It was a quiet time as the skipper and crew were eating. He lit a cigarette and pushed back comfortably in the skipper's well-upholstered chair.

Among the electronic equipment on the bridge were two radios. One picked up the messages passed from ship to ship, constantly bombarding the bridge with voices from Iceland, Britain, Germany and Denmark. The other remained silent, permanently tuned to the international distress frequency.

As he dozed after a long, hard day Oddsson was brought suddenly to attention by a voice which burst from the hitherto silent second set. Hurriedly he picked up a pencil and grabbed a sheet of paper to write down the message…

'Mayday, Mayday, Mayday. It is the British trawler *St Romanus* from Hull. We are leaving now.' The voice then gave the position of 63.5 degrees north and 0.4 west. Or at least that was what Oddsson thought it said. Although repeated, there was doubt as to the exact position. Was it 0.4 west? Or could it have been 4.0 west?

Tense now, Oddsson listened intently as the link faded. Then he heard it, a second voice. He believed it was British, a trawler trying to contact *St Romanus*. The voices faded, the set returned to silence.

Oddsson thought fast. By his reckoning the vessel was about 800 miles from *Vikingur 111*. He reported what he heard to the skipper.

Fourteen days later Thordur Oddsson listened to another radio message. It told him of the loss of the Hull trawler *St Romanus*.

REYKJAVIK, ICELAND, 14 JANUARY 1968

It was midnight and as the Icelandic capital slept the *Kingston Peridot* slipped into port.

She did not remain there long, just long enough to put ashore William Good, the vessel's cook, who had been injured in heavy seas as she made her way northwards.

It had happened suddenly. As the *Peridot* ploughed into a trough of water he lost his footing and plunged down a companionway, receiving severe bruising to his head and chest. Skipper Ray Wilson had little choice but to put him ashore.

'I wanted to carry on, but they told me I would not be fit for several days,' he said.

Skipper Wilson was soon back at sea. Mr Good stayed three days in Iceland before being sent home.

ST ANDREW'S DOCK, HULL, 20 JANUARY 1968

Everything was in order.

Final checks by the ship's husband showed that all the crew were on board, hands were called to their stations and the ropes cast off. Slowly, cautiously the *Ross Cleveland* inched her way past the line of tied-up trawlers and out of the lockpit. A few friends gathered to watch her leave, shouting farewells to their mates as she crept into the Humber.

Built in Aberdeen by John Lewis and Sons Ltd in 1949 for Hudson Brothers Trawlers, of Hull, she was 659 tons, carried 20 men and was a good sea ship.

With a final blast of farewell she jutted down the Humber, soon to be lost from view to the watchers on the shore. And she sailed into fishing industry history.

THE *Hull Daily Mail* NEWSROOM, 12.40PM, 24 JANUARY 1968

Beneath a huge map of the East Riding Charles Levitt swayed precariously on the back legs of the captain's chair behind the green metal newsdesk, chewed on a sandwich and carefully perused the columns of market prices in the *Financial Times*.

For once the phones were quiet, the room peaceful as the morning rush was over. Deep below in the bowels of this gaunt red brick building, purpose-built for the *Mail* in the 1920s, came the first rumble of the presses as they began to roll, pumping out the day's first edition and gradually picking up speed to send vibrations throughout the labyrinthine corridors of a building which took up most of one side of Jameson Street.

It was not a particularly inspiring work of architecture, but on one point none could argue – it was certainly built to last. Hitler's bombs had destroyed neighbouring Hammonds. At the *Mail* not a wall was even cracked.

Equally good survivors were its presses, giant rotaries installed 40 years earlier after being bought from the *News of the World*. In a single afternoon these noisy giants would spew out over 135,000 newspapers to be delivered to homes in an area which went as far as Scarborough in the north and Goole in the west.

In the heart of the building lay the nerve centre of the *Mail's* newsgathering operations. Once the office of a former editor, who had, it was claimed, hanged himself there, it was wood panelled, grubby and untidy. The parquet floor had certainly seen better days, the walls had lost their gloss for ever, and were now covered with tattered memos, stuck there with fish glue normally used to parcel up newspapers for distribution. Around the perimeter of the room were in-built desks with hardboard tops. Telephone wires trailed across them and the floor.

Among his peers Charles Levitt was regarded as a no-nonsense journalist, a tough taskmaster who knew exactly what he wanted and how to get it. His enthusiasm for the job was undeniable and unshakeable. Today, as always, he wore his trademark yellow pullover and brown suede shoes, now resting on the desktop, as he tilted back in his chair and considered the stock market prices.

There were two other people in the room with him, one a young reporter assigned lunch duty, which meant an hour of making routine telephone calls to the emergency services, and an older, balding man who occupied the desk at the far end to Levitt's.

Smoking on the pipe which never seemed to leave his mouth from the moment he entered the office, the floor around his chair was littered with spent matches. Glasses perched on the end of his nose, he tilted his head back to study what he was writing on the battered Royal typewriter. He was Ernest 'Tim' Underwood, the paper's chief reporter and its fishing correspondent.

The calm was broken by the shrilling of telephone extension 40. Swiftly he unhooked it, greeted the caller and began to make rapid shorthand notes on a scrap of copy paper.

The call over, he rose and walked the length of the room to the newsdesk. What he told Charles Levitt soon had the news editor back in action.

Thirty minutes later the *Mail's* second edition was on the streets. It carried a story which bore the headline: 'Not heard of for 11 days. Hunt for silent Hull Trawler'. It was a carefully constructed piece, written with the greatest care so as not to cause undue alarm.

It said: 'All ships and aircraft were this afternoon alerted to keep watch in the North Sea for a Hull trawler which has not been heard of for 11 days. The 600 tons *St Romanus* was last reported seen off the Lofoten Islands on 13 January by another Hull trawler, the *St Matthew*.

'While the trawler's silence is officially regarded as no more than a radio failure, a full-scale air and sea search has begun'.

And from Mr Jonathan Watson Hall, a director of the owning company, came a statement saying there was no need for anxiety. It was, he said, a routine precaution to send a message to shipping after they were unable to make contact.

The *Mail* used the report on page one. Charles Levitt put a note onto the reporters' daily diary for a follow-up story the next day.

24 January 1968, HM Coastguard Station, Wick

FROM C.G. ABERDEEN TO C.G. WICK. WICK PRIORITY PASS WICK RADIO, D.O.S. KIRKWALL, LERWICK AND WICK. FOLLOWING RECEIVED FROM C.G. CROMER. FOLLOWING RECEIVED FROM D.O. FLAMBOROUGH. PLEASE BROADCAST THE FOLLOWING TO ALL SHIPS, BEGINS PAN. INFORMATION IS REQUESTED OF STEAM TRAWLER ST ROMANUS REF NO H 223. DESCRIPTION BLACK HULL WITH NARROW YELLOW BAND, BROWN GRAINED SUPERSTRUCTURE, TWO MASTS, BLACK FUNNEL WITH WIDE RED

BAND. LAST HEARD OF LOFOTEN ISLAND 13 JANUARY. ANY INFORMATION TO WICK RADIO FOR C.G. CROMER = 231145z.

In the Wick Lookout, Coastguard Henderson picked up the message, studied it and then paused to consider what he had read before acknowledging it. At the time neither he, nor anyone else, had any inclination of what it heralded – the beginning of a number of searches which would have a chain reaction across the northern seas as the days went by. That message was to prove the start of what coastguards would later say was the one of the most intensive and exhaustive searches ever carried out by the North Scotland Division of the service. It was also to be a reminder of a signal received by the service three years earlier, in January 1965, telling of the disappearance of an Aberdeen trawler, the *Blue Crusader*, which was last seen off the Orkneys.

As the search built up for *St Romanus* many began to seriously consider the implications and the definite similarities to that earlier tragedy. To begin with neither vessel had been heard of by its owners for 10 days before any marine lifesaving organisation had been informed.

And both incidents had happened in January, notorious as the worst month for weather conditions in northern waters.

The Pan – a coding which indicates a signal that must be regarded as urgent – was broadcast not only by Wick, but also Bodo Radio in Northern Norway and Reykjavik, Iceland. In Russia, too, there was concern, with Murmansk radio being requested to ask the Soviet fleet fishing in the Barents Sea to keep a look out for *St Romanus*.

And in England the BBC played its part, playing a message during one of its routine shipping weather forecasts at 2pm on the *Light Programme* of Thursday 25 January. It was to no avail.

To the families of trawlermen, death and injury at sea were no strangers. The long and anxious wait for news of loved ones was something with which the fishing industry had lived for generations. Homes across Hull had known the heartache when a knock on the door brought the news that a vessel had been in trouble, that a man had been swept overboard, that a crew had vanished without trace.

So it was with *St Romanus*.

As the city went to sleep that night, in 20 homes there was only the agony of suspense.

Among her crew were two brothers, both in their 20s. One man was the father of seven and another had four children.

There was a 16-year-old boy aboard her, sailing as deckie learner, and his father put into words what the entire fishing industry was thinking: 'We are living on hopes. The waiting is terrible. All we can do is pray that everything will be all right.' His son, he said, was 'mad keen' on fishing.

One young mother of two was only 17 years old. She said her husband had not wanted to make the trip. 'But we were buying our own house – we got it last week – and he went to get the money for furniture.'

And the waiting went on…and on…

HULL, 25 JANUARY 1968

The rules were clearly laid down. Trawlers at sea should report each day their position and give details of their catch.

It did not happen that way with *St Romanus*.

For she did not report at all.

As tension built up in 20 Hull homes concern mounted on St Andrew's Dock in the offices of Thomas Hamling and Co. But still the firm clung on to the hope that all was well.

In fact, 12 days after the vessel left, the owners were still maintaining an optimistic stance. After asking all shipping to keep a routine look-out for the vessel a statement from them said: 'Until about 2 February, when the *St Romanus* is due home, she will be within the limits of a normal voyage. About then we should start to worry, but until then we do not think there is any cause for anxiety.'

The company's policy was also clearly laid down on another issue – that of radio operators being carried aboard its vessels. It was the habit of the owners to provide on their vessels, wherever possible, a man qualified as a radio operator. When *St Romanus* sailed no such officer was available to sail with her and in accordance with agreements with trade unions an extra deckhand was carried instead. The radio would be the responsibility of the skipper who had a radio telephone certificate awarded to him two years earlier after an examination by Board of Trade radio surveyors.

Two days after she sailed, Hamlings sent a message to her in the form of a telegram via Wick Radio asking Skipper Wheeldon to report her position.

What no one had any idea of at that time was that she had probably already vanished.

For four days Wick Radio continued to call, but to no avail. And the owners hung on and waited, unaware of one vital piece of information – that a life raft had been found.

In fact no one at that time appreciated that the raft was from *St Romanus*. It had been discovered fully inflated on 13 January by a Danish fishing vessel. But it was not reported to the vessel's base in Esbjerg until 20 January. The only other evidence that *St Romanus* had sunk came on 21 February when a lifebuoy from the vessel was found on a beach near Hirshals in the north of Denmark.

THE NORTH SEA OFF THE LOFOTEN ISLANDS, 26 JANUARY 1968

Below them, the waves.

The lone Shackleton aircraft from No. 120 Squadron flew low as it wound its way back to Ballykelly.

Its crew were tired after hours of fruitlessly searching a vast area of empty sea. In a radio message to the nerve centre of the search headquarters at Pitreavie Castle in Scotland the aircraft's pilot radioed the terse message: 'Nothing to report.'

Other aircraft, too, became involved. Planes from Icelandair, Scandinavian Airlines and others were given a full description of the missing trawler with instructions to report any vessel resembling it. They saw nothing.

On the surface, buffeted by high winds, a flotilla of ships scoured mile after mile of emptiness. Led by the fisheries protection frigate HMS *Grafton*, warships of the Norwegian Navy, fishing vessels and aircraft scoured up to 2,800 square miles of sea a day. Their efforts proved fruitless.

So, too, did continued attempts to call the missing vessel on radio.

The search by now included at least 20 British trawlers, Norwegian fishing boats and amphibious aircraft from the Royal Norwegian Air Force.

And still there was nothing.

In Hull the fishing industry's welfare officer, Mr Claude Weissenbourne, and Superintendent David MacMillan of the Royal National Mission to Deep Sea Fishermen went from house to house telling the crew's families what was known.

And a spokesman for the owners said: 'We are assuming nothing as a result of finding the life raft. The search for the ship goes on.'

It was, said one coastguard, 'like looking for a matchstick in a pond'.

At the Fishermen's Mission in Hull prayers were said as the search continued. But time was ticking quickly away…

THE *HULL DAILY MAIL* NEWSROOM, 29 JANUARY 1968

Bob Wellings had been the paper's shipping correspondent for more years than he cared to remember. It was a job he loved and one which earned him respect and praise from all sectors of that industry.

He lit a Senior Service and perused the somewhat dull columns of the shipping newspaper *Lloyd's List* before pulling on a yellow and ageing telephone headset and starting to make his daily calls for the latest developments in the hunt for the missing vessel.

It was becoming a regular routine and one which had to be completed by 10.45am at the latest, giving him just enough time to write a story for the first edition for he was a fast writer, and an accurate one.

As he moved down his list of contacts connected with *St Romanus* – all written inside the cover of a battered brown file – he spoke to, among others, Jack Ashwell, a local official of the Transport and General Workers' Union, which had a branch for fishermen, although they were difficult men to organise, having jobs which were regarded as casual and therefore rather insecure, and never being at home long enough to find time for union matters.

It turned out to be a conversation that not only made the *Mail's* front page that night, but one which was to have considerable impact in shaping events which were to follow.

As Wellings made his calls Hull North MP Kevin McNamara was reading the morning papers as his train pulled into London's King's Cross station. McNamara was a member of the TGWU and had been well briefed by them. He had also spoken to the relatives of five *St Romanus* crewmen who lived in his constituency. As a result he had points to make and questions to ask – if he could arrive at the Commons in time to table them for emergency answer that day.

As McNamara neared London and Wellings began to write his story, high above the turbulent waters of the North Sea United States fighters and reconnaissance aircraft were joining the hunt for *St Romanus*. On the sea, ships of several nations combed a vast area. And still they found nothing.

Ashwell and McNamara wanted an investigation into several key points:

1. Why was there delay in reporting the discovery of a life raft until several days after it had been found?

2. Why the alarm was not raised earlier in Hull?

3. Whether it was true that a wireless operator refused to serve in the vessel, as had been claimed by the Hull district secretary of the radio operators' union. Men were said to dislike the vessel – and other similar trawlers built for Belgian owners – because the chartroom, radio equipment and operator's berth were all in one, which prevented the operator, who worked up to 17 hours a day, actually getting any sleep. It had been raised with trawler owners, but so far nothing had been done to tackle the problem.

4. Why it took 10 days to discover that an alleged radio message from *St Romanus* was picked up off Iceland by *Vikingur III*.

5. Why there was delay in reporting the distress signal on 12 January and why it did not arrive until the previous week.

That afternoon Mr J.P. Mallalieu, Minister of State at the Board of Trade, told the Commons: 'We shall certainly have an investigation the moment that, unhappily, we are forced to assume the vessel is lost.'

Back in Hull Mr Watson Hall put the finishing touches to a letter which was sent to every family who had a man aboard the missing vessel.

It said: 'Her safety cannot be ruled out, but chances of finding her are now very slight.'

The letter mentioned 'fading hopes of better news' and added: 'The search continues, but the prospect of finding any survivors is now so remote that we cannot encourage you with hope…We are deeply distressed over the appalling loss of life caused by this unexplained tragedy to a well found ship, and wish to send you our heartfelt sympathy in your anxiety.'

Four days later came the news that the families of men aboard *St Romanus* had dreaded.

A knock on the door brought them face to face with Mr McMillan, who told them that there was now no hope at all. The vessel must be considered lost.

It was the day she should have returned home.

THE SKAGAGRUNN, NORTH ICELAND, 26 JANUARY 1968

The weather was bad – and getting worse. The *Kingston Peridot* rolled and pitched as she sailed head-on into a biting wind. As the day progressed so the gale increased. From force six it mounted relentlessly in its ferocity, increasing to force nine.

Earlier, as a bleak dawn cracked through the heavy banks of cloud to bring the cheerless daytime twilight of northern waters, Skipper Wilson ordered the trawl to be shot at about 7am, but the brake on the winch slacked off 13 lengths – all the warp – and had to be hauled.

Such was the situation almost four hours later when Skipper Wilson spoke to his friend and fellow skipper Bill Ward, of the *Kingston Sardius*, which was fishing on Iceland's north-east coast.

AFFIDAVIT OF SKIPPER WILLIAM WARD, *KINGSTON SARDIUS*

'The fact that Skipper Wilson was stowing the trawl below indicated that the weather was bad and he expected worse, as he also said to me that he intended to steam towards me and fish again. One would not normally stow the trawl below when intending to fish again within the next twenty-four hours.

'He also informed me he would have to chop ice before he steamed. It was about 11.10 when I finished speaking to him and my understanding then was that he intended to chop ice for a couple of hours and then steam towards me.

'At about 19.00 my radio operator picked up a routine telegram destined for the *Kingston Peridot* in the Wick traffic list. About 19.45 I told my operator to call the *Kingston Peridot* and pass the message to him. The radio operator and myself called him continually from 19.45 to 20.30, but could not raise him, and at intervals through the night until 11.45 on the 27th the operator called him, but was still unable to raise him.

'I was on the bridge all night looking after my ship in the now heavy weather. I was not too happy about having been unable to raise *Kingston Peridot*, particularly as he had said he would contact me when he got nearer and the weather conditions were bad.

'At 08.00 on the 27th I told the radio operator to try again but our aerials were iced up and we were not getting much of a reading…'

Together with another vessel, the *Boston Weelsby*, Skipper Ward continued to call the *Kingston Peridot* throughout the following day, but without success. At about 13.00 hours on 28 January he received a message from the owners addressed to all their vessels in the area telling them to keep a lookout for the *Kingston Peridot*. Nothing was seen or heard.

HESSLE ROAD, HULL, 29 JANUARY 1968

She was, reported one columnist, 'a tough, tenacious battleaxe, a cannon of a woman'.

It may have reflected the public view of Lilian Bilocca. The private side was somewhat different.

Certainly she was as down to earth as any other Hessle-Roader, and definitely not afraid to speak her mind. Yet behind the often aggressive facade of this 17 stone amazon lay a soft centre.

With a 21-year-old son – Ernie – in trawlers and husband Charlie a merchant seaman Lil knew as much as anyone about the hazards of going to sea and the waiting and hoping that all too often came with it for those who remained on shore. Fishing was not an occupation she would have wished her son to undertake. And she also worried about her daughter Virginia. 'If she marries a trawlerman, it'll break my heart,' she told friends.

The drama of the *St Romanus* played on her mind as she worked in a Hessle Road fish factory where the gravity of the situation had a calming effect on the usually noisy workers. As she thought more and more about it there developed something else, the stirring of anger that fishermen were generally treated badly, had little formal representation, and a job which was never secure as they were regarded as casual workers. And it was work which put them face to face with some of the worst weather in the world, an occupation which had a higher death and accident rate than any other. If they would not fight for themselves, she reasoned, then someone else would have to.

Armed with a few sheets of paper, a pen and great deal of determination Lilian Bilocca went to 'war' against some of the most powerful names in the fishing industry. It was to make her and those who supported her national figures.

The word spread rapidly. Information was at a premium. Newspapers were bought, read, re-read and then read again before being passed on. Truth became embellished as gossip fuelled new stories. Two vessels missing. Thoughts turned back to the loss of the *Lorella* and *Roderigo*. Hessle Road remembered. And prayed.

Hessle Road WAS the Hull fishing industry. As one grew so did the other. The four-mile stretch which linked Hull with Hessle, a country lane in the mid-19th century, was, 100 years later, one of the most densely populated areas of the city. And then as now, it was strictly working class and proud of the fact. What it has lacked in architectural style it has gained in humanity.

A hundred years earlier builders had embarked on an orgy of house building to cater for the growing number of workers who sailed the fast-growing trawler fleet or were employed in the shore-based industries which kept vessels at sea and processed their catches. Hessle Road was built on fish.

In the early days of fishing from Hull smack owners used Albert Dock, but even after its expansion into William Wright Dock in 1880 it proved too small to cater for the growing number of vessels, one problem being that the smacks were forced to share berthing facilities with merchant vessels. The need for a proper fish dock was great. As a result St Andrew's Dock opened in 1883 and was extended just four years later. The fishing industry had at last a proper home of its own.

With this came a wave of development. Railways, fishing and dock work all required labour. Hessle Road provided it, becoming one of busiest thoroughfares in Hull. It was later to be described as 'a village within a city'. It remained an apt description.

It was that closeness, that shared anxiety, which helped fuel a campaign which was to attract nationwide attention. It was triggered when Lilian Bilocca took her pad and pen along Hessle Road on a cold and busy Friday afternoon. Her aim – to take to trawler owners the views of the fishing community and others on safety measures for men at sea. In particular she was concerned that the *St Romanus* had sailed without a radio operator. There was nothing illegal in that, for the skipper was adequately qualified to handle all communications. But in her view this was just not good enough. Others soon began to see her point. The scene was set for one of the most remarkable campaigns in British industrial history.

THE ICELANDIC COAST, 26-29 JANUARY 1968

The message went out just after midday on 26 January via Wick Radio to three trawlers from the Hellyer Brothers fleet warning them not to return to Hull for Friday's market as the previous two Fridays had seen a strike by bobbers and there was reason to believe the same thing may happen again. Two vessels received the message but Wick Radio failed to clear the one destined for *Kingston Peridot*.

The following day, at about the same time, the radio operator on the *Kingston Sardius* attempted to contact the *Peridot* but failed. At 11.00 hours the skipper sent via Wick Radio a telegram to the owners reporting his position and telling them that weather conditions were worsening. The wind was northerly and it was freezing hard.

And as the hours passed conditions grew worse and worse. In the area around Grimsey Island where the *Peridot* had been fishing the storms were said to be the worst for 13 years.

It was a message timed 5.20pm on 30 January from Lloyd's agent in Reykjavik which produced the first real clue that something had gone seriously wrong. He reported to the Mutual Insurance Society in Hull that reports in local newspapers were telling of a heavy oil slick in Axafjordar and that a partially deflated life raft had been found and identified as belonging to the missing vessel.

Immediately a search was mounted by the National Lifesaving Association of Iceland under its superintendent, Mr Hannes Hafstein. A land search was complemented by the use of small craft and a coastguard vessel and later by a Shackleton aircraft from Kinloss. And as the search continued with the volunteer Icelandic force battling against appalling weather, more evidence came to light. Three lifebuoys marked *Kingston Peridot* were found, as were two containers with signal flares, hatch planks, a port side lantern and trawl bobbin.

And three months later, on 22 April, came further proof that the vessel had foundered when the Icelandic trawler *Saethor* discovered a ventilator cowl in her net. Experts were later to assert that they were certain that the cowl came from the *Kingston Peridot*.

THE *ROSS CLEVELAND*, NORTHERN ICELAND, 29 JANUARY 1968

It was not going well.

From the start the trip had been difficult for both trawler and men. Skipper Phil Gay, an experienced and competent seaman with a good track record had not found the going at all easy.

First there was the weather. He had sailed for the north-eastern coast of Iceland and began fishing on 25 January, but was forced to stop when the weather became unfavourable. Moving across the top of the island the vessel next began fishing off the north-west corner of Iceland. Again the weather proved a major problem. Fishing ceased.

Skipper Gay faced another dilemma, too. His cook, Bill Howbrigg was unwell, and apparently growing steadily worse. Difficulties with his breathing became ever more acute, and with pneumonia the most likely diagnosis there was no alternative but to head into Reykjavik to put him ashore.

THE *HULL DAILY MAIL* NEWSROOM

The list had just 20 names and addresses. They were those of the skipper and crew of the *St Romanus*. It was a moment those involved in covering the trawler story had dreaded. It was time to visit and interview relatives of men who must now be presumed missing and most likely dead.

Popular mythology paints the journalist as a hard-nosed, interfering, foot-in-the-door merchant who will do anything for a story and to hell with the consequences.

That is a fallacy.

Charles Levitt knew it only too well as he carefully studied the single sheet of paper in his hand and pondered who should call on whom. It was not an easy task.

His choice of reporters made, Levitt summoned them to the newsdesk and gave his orders.

There was to be no pestering relatives. No pushing people into giving statements against their will. Reporters were to politely ask for an interview and a photograph of crewmen from the vessel. If families wanted to give them, then fine. If not, then that was that.

Three reporters were despatched. Each was in no doubt as to what was wanted, or to what the approach should be…

Stuart Russell recalls an assignment for the *Hull Daily Mail,* January 1968.

'There is no doubt that this was the most difficult day we had yet faced. It's one thing asking trawler firms, union men and dock workers for their comments. It's another thing entirely coming face to face with people who may – or may not – have been bereaved.

'Strangely it was to prove much easier than I at least would have even guessed.

'Trawler families knew we would call. One or two even rang the office to ask when we were going round. It was part of the process, a few paragraphs and a picture in the paper was expected. It was part of coming to terms with the tragedy of it all. But even when we were welcomed into homes it was still never easy.

'People would have photographs waiting for us, they would select the one they liked the best and ask us to use that one. We usually did, providing it was of good enough quality to print.

'Once we had used the picture it was kept in the office safe until it was returned. It was all too easy for a passport-sized photograph to get lost and we all dreaded that happening.

'People were very good, extremely brave and composed. You felt as if you were intruding at times, but they never berated you for that, they accepted you were there to do your job and they were usually willing to co-operate. Along with my colleague Derek Hilton, who also worked on the *Mail*, I knocked on many doors in that period and was always well received. But it was never easy. It was something you did because you were told to. You wouldn't have done it out of choice.'

VICTORIA HALL, HESSLE ROAD, HULL, 2 FEBRUARY 1968

Collecting signatures on a petition was one thing. Forcing people in authority to listen and then act was another. Lilian Bilocca decided it was time for action and set about creating it.

The venue was Victoria Hall, a decaying, gloomy relic of better days tucked away off an alley which ran between a shop and St Barnabas Church. On a miserable Friday afternoon an estimated 600 people, most of them women, packed into this cold and musty building. Harsh, unshaded light bounced off green and cream walls, Children scampered around the peripheral of the crowd. Babies in prams squealed for attention, dogs raced through the forest of legs. At the front, directly in front of the stage, the press corps assembled, by now more than 30 strong. Fishing was becoming national news.

A white-coated Mrs Bilocca called the meeting to order. She was their leader and she told them straight what she thought and what they should do. It was an impressive performance.

'Right, lasses, we're here to talk about what we're going to do after the losses of these trawlers. I don't want any of you effin' and blindin'. Remember the press and TV are here. We want an orderly meeting...'

She was prepared to go to jail if it would help win better and safer conditions for men on trawlers. 'I intend to see Harold Wilson [then Prime Minister] next week and I won't come back until I have seen him,' she bellowed. It met with mass approval.

Many others wanted their say, too. Among them was the father of a young trawlerman lost on the *St Romanus*, who accused vessel owners of thinking only of 'fat profits' and not of their crews.

For one man there was a loud cheer as he stepped onto the stage to tell the meeting that his union – the National Union of Seamen – supported them all the way in their fight against trawler owners who were 'in the same mould' as ship owners. John Prescott, later to become MP for East Hull and 29 years later Deputy Prime Minister, added: 'For too long the seamen have been second-rate citizens.'

There was sympathy from James Johnson, MP for West Hull, whose constituency included the fish dock and who admitted to being 'intensely shocked' at the losses.

As speaker after speaker took to the stage cries came of 'march on the dock. Let the owners have it'. In the highly charged atmosphere it reflected exactly what most thought must happen.

They filed out within minutes, angry, emotional, determined and united. More than half the audience, a crocodile of pram pushing, shouting women and bawling children marched along Hessle Road, down West Dock Street and under the subway onto St Andrew's Dock. Anxious dock police made a vain attempt to halt the march which swept past and on to the offices of Hull Steam Trawlers Mutual Insurance Company, Mrs Bilocca entered to demand a meeting with owners of the missing vessels.

After some discussion it was agreed a deputation could go in. Accompanied by fellow campaigners Mrs Rose Cooper and Mrs Mavis Wilkinson, Mrs Bilocca presented a six-point safety charter in a 50-minute meeting – but not with the men they wanted to see. They had declined the opportunity to attend. Instead the demands were made to Michael Burton, chairman of the Hull Fishing Vessel Owners Association, Mr Lionel Cox, its secretary, and Rear Admiral John Ievers, manager of the insurance company.

White-coated Mrs Bilocca came out unimpressed. 'There's only one way to make these people meet us and hear our case and that's by taking action,' she declared to the waiting crowd. A few hours later she was to put those words into practice.

THE EVENING OF 2 FEBRUARY 1968

The initial fury had died down. On a cheerless evening a second meeting began to discuss the response of trawler owners. And new faces began to come to the fore.

One of those involved was no stranger to being in the limelight. She was Yvonne Marie Blenkinsop, a pretty 28-year-old cabaret singer in Hull clubland and mother of three who went onto a very different kind of stage and delivered a stinging attack on the dangers which she said beset the men of the Hull fishing fleet. Yvonne knew only too well the anguish which faced many of her audience of 200 trawlermen's wives and girlfriends. Only four years before she had been in a similar position when her father, himself a fisherman, was lost at sea.

In the harsh lights of the damp and dingy hall, many of those present stamping their feet in a vain attempt to keep warm, Yvonne Marie – her stage name in clubland – gave a stirring performance, urging the women of Hull to take their fight to the Prime Minister if necessary. As for going to sea – no one would make her do it, not for a million pounds a week. 'Our men are fools with hearts of gold to do it,' she said. It was a sentiment which was well received.

Also speaking that night was 30-year-old Mary Denness, whose husband was sailing as mate on the Grimsby trawler *Ross Vanguard*. She was angry, too, and urged united action, condemning as 'wrong' the entire system of trawling. She urged that the time a man had to serve on deck before being allowed to take his ticket should be lengthened to improve his experience.

Honest and open as the women were other people in the room were there to further ends which were far removed from the fishermen's case.

Politically motivated elements were creeping into the whole affair – and among them came the views of a Hull university lecturer who lashed out at the whole business of trawling, describing the vessels as 'coffins' sent out despite the dangers 'because a lot of profit is involved'.

Politics, however, were most certainly not in the heart or mind of Robert Dockerty that night. He was the father of 16-year-old Robert Dockerty of the *St Romanus*. And he bitterly criticised the Royal Navy, which had only short time earlier turned out in force to search for a missing French submarine.

'But they never looked for my lad…he was just a mere tool. I loved my boy and he loved the sea,' he said.

On that sobering thought the meeting dispersed, but its impact was to turn into dramatic action just a few hours later.

St Andrew's Dock, Hull, 3 February 1968

Huddled in a draughty doorway in a vain attempt to keep warm, the reporters waited, tired, cold and hungry. The night was black and bitter with snow flurries sweeping across the vastness of the dock on which the trawlers rocked, gently straining at their moorings. The lights reflected on the icy pavements, the silence almost eerie as the long hours ticked by.

Some crewmen arrived early to board their vessels, due to sail shortly after dawn. One carried crates with bottles of ale, dropping two of them as he stumbled up the plank and onto his boat. Cursing, he probed the black waters with a boat hook, but to no avail.

In this dank and cheerless place there was no shelter, nowhere to find a drink or sandwich. The reporters shivered and cursed. It was, as they had feared, becoming a long night.

The reason for their vigil lay several hours back, shortly after the meeting in the Victoria Hall broke up and Lilian Bilocca and her supporters announced that they would be on the dock 'first thing' to stop any more vessels leaving. It was all they could do and they were determined to do it.

Night slowly became day, the grey dawn of early February shrugging its way through thick cloud. And the waiting went on. On any weekday morning the dock would have been bustling with activity from the early hours. It was different at the weekend. There was no fish market and the offices of trawler owners and other business were closed. The dock was calm and peaceful, its customary noise silenced. Even the infamous Lollipop Shop, with its range of 'top shelf' magazines was closed. There was no business on a Saturday.

But this particular weekend there was activity of a different kind. At the lockhead they began to gather, a handful of women, a battalion of reporters and photographers, hangers-on and police. As the trawler *St Keverne* inched its way through and into the Humber the resentment and anger spilled over into dramatic action.

With Lilian Bilocca were other campaigners equally determined to prevent vessels from going to sea and to highlight the dangers which faced fishermen. They included Mrs Rose Cooper and Mrs Mary Pye, whose husband Herbert was on the *St Romanus*. And that same day one of Mrs Pye's five sons – Albert – was due to sail from Hull as mate on the *Ross Aquila*.

Confrontation came when Mrs Bilocca demanded to know if the *St Keverne* was carrying a radio operator. Crewmen told her she was not. Grimly determined, she attempted to stop the vessel leaving, desperately trying to jump onto its deck, but was restrained by police. As the vessel cleared the lockhead women shouted and screamed in a futile bid to stop her going down the Humber. It was to no avail, but it had helped hammer home their point. Yet there was a touch of disappointment as Mrs Bilocca gave her comments to the assembled Press. Many more women had promised to be present when they had met the night before, but only a handful had turned out. It was, nevertheless, a performance which grabbed attention. National newspapers, radio and television began to look closer into the problems facing fishermen at sea. And one Sunday tabloid reporter came up with a new name for Mrs Bilocca – Big Lil.

As the women's protest was played out at the lockhead, another, quieter, but equally determined, demonstration was taking place nearby. Among the lines of moored trawlers one should have sailed on that morning's tide. She was the *St Andronicus*, a sister vessel to *St Romanus*. But as preparations were being made to for her to leave, confrontation came. The crew refused to sail her…

It began over the state of the life jackets. True, the vessel carried them, enough to cater for every man. The trouble was, according to the crew, they were just not good enough. The problem had started 24 hours earlier when similar complaints were lodged. The vessel failed to make that day's tide.

On *St Andronicus* men demanded that union officials look into their complaints. They would sail only when their representatives were convinced that the life jackets carried were of the type approved by the Board of Trade.

The controversy fuelled an already heated situation. But much worse was still to come.

ISAFJORDUR, ICELAND, SUNDAY 4 FEBRUARY 1968

They had sought shelter 24 hours earlier after receiving a weather forecast which gave no room for argument or discussion. Things were looking distinctly bad. The high cliffs on either side of the deeply cut fjord should have offered good protection. As the gales whipped up to hurricane force with blizzards raking across the turbulent water, they dodged into the teeth of the wind. And waited.

Not only the *Ross Cleveland* had run for shelter. Several other vessels from Hull and Grimsby were there too. Fishing was suspended. The winds shrieked through the rigging, snow lashed across decks which were becoming thicker and thicker with ice, and men worked feverishly to clear it, sweating with physical effort despite the intense cold.

Some of the vessels in the sheltering fleet were probably in a better position than others. They had arrived earlier than the rest of the pack and had managed to lay up in some of the smaller fjords which adjoined the main waterway. But some, because of a lack of room in which to anchor and seek shelter, were compelled to lie and dodge in the main fjord, as *Ross Cleveland* had done. There was nothing else to do.

And the weather grew worse.

The trawler fleet was receiving reports four times a day in Morse code from the Icelandic Meteorological Service. For vessels which had no radio operator a radio telephone service was available and frequently used by British trawlers for getting a reliable and regular service from Reykjavik.

And still the weather grew worse.

Chopping the ice became impossible for crews could not operate in conditions which were by now said to be the worst in three decades.

Skipper Len Whur, then in command of the *Kingston Andalusite*, was among those weathering the storm. He said later he had never known trawlers ice up as badly. One or two were in such a critical condition that their crews had to heave their gear overboard to clear the deck as the ice was level with the rails and casing.

He had seen ice before on many occasions, forming in even a force four wind. But this was the worst he had ever encountered. He was to say later: 'I have never seen ships in the state they were in Isafjord in the icy conditions at that time…I have fished in the same ship in force seven and eight winds and taken water and never heeled over like we did in those conditions.'

On shore, Icelanders who dared to venture from their homes were unable to stand in the gales ,which were by now at hurricane force – 120mph – and were forced to crawl. Houses became covered with ice 40–50cm thick. A radio beacon, wireless aerials, power lines and telephone lines crashed to earth as the storm reached its peak, covering fence posts with 23cm of ice. And with it came more blizzards, sweeping down from the north-north-east. The seas were mountainous, even in the fjord, the surf lashing the shoreline and bringing with it haddock, catfish and shellfish, the first time this had been known to happen since 7 and 8 February 1925.

The *Ross Cleveland*, Isafjord, Iceland, 4 February 1968

On the rails the ice built up relentlessly. On the decks, the hatches and the bridge the blizzards deposited an ever-thickening carpet of white. The wind screamed as it tore down the fjord, whipping the waters into creamy foam.

And men fought a desperate battle to save their ship.

Mate Harry Eddom was later to recall: 'We used axes to get it off and were kicking it off. We had to use axes to break it off the ship's sides. There is no specified equipment. There are axes, battens from the ice room, big spanners…anything that will knock ice off.'

All day they fought to chop the ice, splitting into teams of two men on the whaleback, two on the winches and two working down the sides. Ice re-formed as quickly as it was chipped off.

And the battle went on. And on…

A continual problem for Skipper Gay as he fought to keep the vessel on a steady course, dodging into the gale, was that of ice on the radar scanner. Even when men had to leave the deck because conditions were too bad to work it was vital to have the radar functioning. Eddom was dressed to carry out the task, wearing long cotton underpants, but no vest, a khaki shirt, moleskin trousers, thick jersey knee-length stockings, a 'duck' suit of plastic material consisting of trousers and smock-type cover made for him and Dunlop thigh boots. It was to prove sufficient to save his life.

When the end came it was swift, decisive and dramatic. There was no warning. Communications were severely limited. Despite the fact that other vessels were within a short distance no one could do anything. The *Ross Cleveland* died alone, but in the company of friends.

At about 23.30 hours the *Kingston Andalusite*, which was two cables to starboard, was asked to pass information obtained from her radar to the *Ross Cleveland*.

The *Ross Cleveland* had just 10 minutes to live.

From the report of the inquiry into the loss of *Ross Cleveland*, concerning events in Isafjord on Thursday 30 January 1969:

'Just as the *Ross Cleveland's* radar had got into operation again, the *Ross Cleveland* and the *Kingston Andalusite* which had been laid with the wind on her starboard side, determined to get head to wind and dodge across to the eastern side of the fjord in order to avoid being set aground on the western side. With her wheel hard-a-starboard and with engines working at half speed ahead the skipper of the *Ross Cleveland* endeavoured to bring his vessel head into the wind. She, however, failed to respond. The engines were rung at full speed ahead and the *Ross Cleveland* heeled over to port and lay on her port side, capsized and sank in a position some three miles off Arnanes Light…'

On the *Kingston Andalusite*, Skipper Whur looked on in horror as the blip on the radar screen vanished.

Seconds before, across a quarter of a mile of hurricane-lashed water, came the final dramatic message from the stricken vessel. He had shouted into the radio a desperate message: 'Keep her going full speed, Phil and keep up with me.'

'I was going full speed ahead to the wind and keeping radar watch for the *Cleveland* and myself as we were going to dodge before we laid. Then Phil shouted "Help us Len, she's going" and we stood looking out of the bridge window and watched him. We saw his lights and the horizontal lights on the bridge went vertical and all of a sudden they were out. I looked on the radar and saw no echo whatever on the port beam. We called *Ross Cleveland* several times on VHF and got no reply whatever. We saw the ship turn over and lost her on our radar screen.'

A short time later the news was relayed to trawler owner Charles Hudson at his home near Hull. He poured himself a large brandy and prepared for a long night.

In the streets of Hull the last stragglers from the clubs and pubs picked their way home on frosty streets. The city was cold, silent and still.

And in the Royal National Mission to Deep Sea Fishermen David MacMillan prepared to go knocking on doors across the city…

ISAFJORD, ICELAND, 5 FEBRUARY 1968

It took just seconds – some said as few as seven, others estimated 30 – for *Ross Cleveland* to die, vanishing from the radar screens of other vessels which tried in vain to contact her. And as she died, three crewmen began a battle to survive.

Harry Eddom was to later say he had no recollection of how he reached the raft which was to play such a crucial role in what was to prove one of the most remarkable stories ever to come out of the British fishing fleet. It was a question raised at the official hearing into the *Ross Cleveland*'s loss. The report, signed by Judge J.V. Naisby and wreck assessors R.A. Beattie and W.F. Wright, recorded events as seen by the inquiry: 'The mate, who stated that he was in the starboard side of the wheelhouse, said that the vessel heeled over to port and that he was able to get out of the starboard door and climbed aft along the casing where he saw two members of the crew in the process of launching one of the inflatable life rafts.'

And according to a memorandum by Sub Lt H.J. Matthews RN, Surg Cmdr E.E. Mackay RN and Surg Cmdr J.F. Ryan RN, who later interviewed Eddom at the Equipment and Survival Training School at Seafield Park: 'When the trawler heeled over, Eddom followed the third hand out of the bridge and over the side. As he went over, Eddom noted that one of the life rafts was inflating. He has no recollection of how he reached it as his next memory is of being inside the life raft. There was no head injury or other explanation for his amnesia.'

THE COASTGUARD STATION, WICK, MONDAY 5 FEBRUARY 1968

It was a quiet morning after an equally quiet night. The watch had little to report. Things were normal.

It was at precisely seven minutes past six, as the darkness of night still refused to give way to the greyness of a damp and depressing winter morning, that the message came from the Flamborough station. It was short, stark and dramatic: 'HULL TRAWLER ROSS CLEVELAND REPORTED THREE MILES OFF ARDENES IN ISAFJORD DEEPS, ICELAND, DISAPPEARED OFF RADAR SCREEN AT 0020 HOURS. BLOWING FULL GALE.'

The report had originated from the Icelandic Coastguard vessel *Odinn* and from trawlers in the vicinity of Isafjord. And it triggered a spate of messages, said by one coastguard to have been received 'with frightening rapidity'.

THE *HULL DAILY MAIL*, MONDAY 5 FEBRUARY 1968

Pandora's Box was full and for the reporters that meant a less than inspiring start to the week.

The box, a battered grey file, had received its name years before. It contained news cuttings, invitations and documentation which required working on that day. It was, some wag had maintained, the container of all evil. On a grey and miserable Monday it was a fitting description.

As the newsroom began to fill with people, its musty atmosphere quickly becoming heavy with smoke, Charles Levitt gave instructions to the reporters covering the trawler tragedy. It was to be a busy day, he said. There were likely to be more problems with crews refusing to sail. Mrs Bilocca and other women's leaders had a meeting arranged with trawler owners. Checks were needed with politicians and union officials regarding the mounting campaign for increased safety at sea. There was a lot to do and not a lot of time to do it in.

As the reporters began to shrug off the effects of the weekend and prepare to meet the challenges of a new week, in the adjoining room sub-editor Peter Moore carefully thumbed his way through a pile of overnight copy and began to make decisions on what stories should go where in that evening's edition.

It was a task to which he was no stranger, but today it had assumed greater importance. Recent promotion had seen him appointed deputy chief sub editor and as he stood in for his superior who normally ran the department, this was his first time in control of the paper's production. When Charles Levitt barged through the door, tie slackened off, top shirt button undone and sleeves rolled, his tense voice announcing 'another one's gone' it was received with some degree of scepticism. The sub-editors initially looked on in disbelief as Levitt crisply and hurriedly outlined what was thought to have happened. Within minutes the day's planned pages were scrapped as the paper prepared for a day no one who worked on the paper would ever forget.

St Andrew's Dock, Hull, Monday 5 February 1968

The rumours began to circulate before dawn. By the time Hull went to work the city was buzzing with speculation and gossip.

On the dock a small knot of reporters had gathered outside the offices of Hudson Brothers Trawlers Ltd. They, too, had heard the whispers and told their offices. Reporters in newspaper offices, radio and television stations were putting in calls to northern Iceland, but to no avail. Pressure of demand blocked telephone lines, and some were down because of the storms. The word was that a third Hull trawler had been lost. The stories spread like wildfire, but there was, as yet, no confirmation.

Repeated attempts by the waiting newsmen eventually brought a response from the company. They would not see the whole press pack, just one representative who could then pass information on to the rest. At about 9am veteran *Daily Express* reporter George Hill was elected as spokesman for the 'pack' and made his way through the doors.

HULL DAILY MAIL NEWSROOM

Bob Wellings, a heavy smoker, carefully arranged the items on his desk as he prepared to make his morning round of calls. On the left were his tobacco – St Bruno – his cigarettes – Senior Service – and his matches. On the right the file with his contact numbers. He carefully lit a cigarette, picked up the heavy black telephone headset of extension 49 and dialled.

He, too, had heard the rumours. But that was all they were so far – rumours. It took less than five minutes to confirm they were much more than that.

QUEEN MARY HOSTEL, HULL, 5 FEBRUARY 1968

With a cup of tea in his hand and still wearing a trademark flat cap despite the warmth of the hostel, cook Bill Howbrigg spoke quietly of the ship and the mates he had come to know well, having originally sailed in the latest missing vessel when she was known as *Cape Cleveland*.

At 59 William Leon Howbrigg was no stranger to the sea and to Icelandic waters in particular. He had, after all, sailed for over 40 years. Now, as he sipped hot tea in the hostel which had become his home when ashore – he was unmarried – Howbrigg spoke of his final hours on board. 'It was a good ship. Everybody was happy. Skipper Gay was respected by all. Even when I was aboard, ice was crippling the ship. All hands had to be constantly on deck chipping huge blocks of ice away with axes, spanners or anything they could lay their hands on. Nobody could sleep. It was a living nightmare.

'Skipper Gay wanted to put me ashore two days earlier than he did on 26 January. I carried on working until he told me to rest…'

Before he left, Howbrigg performed one final service for his mates – he baked them bread.

The tragedy was all Hull's. And the nation joined the city in mourning.

The fishing industry was, by tradition, tightly knit, a community on its own which shared it own grief. Now it was joined by tens of thousands of others. Hessle Road had never known anything like it.

But for many there was anger alongside the sorrow. Now 59 men were dead. The fishing community wanted action and it wanted it as a matter of urgency.

The bereaved and the campaigning found their greatest allies were the hordes of pressmen who now scoured the city. Often reviled they now became the fishermen's champions. One national newspaper – the *Daily Telegraph* – summed it up for all:

'Today there were none of the all too familiar groups of relatives huddled around the offices of a trawler company, shivering in the wind and with the emotion of anxiety. Many were wakened by the welfare officer of the Hull Fishing Vessel Owners' Association who broke the news that nothing short of a miracle would bring their menfolk back. For the remainder it was told over breakfast tables or as orphaned children prepared for school.

'Hessle Road and the Fish Dock have gone about their business with that awesome quiet of a community absorbing the unbelievable and, as so many of them in this city learned to do in the wartime blitz, preparing to carry on. Emotion has driven deep, far too deep for dockside demonstrations. Yet, most of even these folk, hardened as they are to disaster, gave way to the relief of tears at the news.

'There can scarcely be a single family now, for these fisherfolk have been close knit for generations, which has not been touched by the tragedies of the *St Romanus, Kingston Peridot* or the *Ross Cleveland.*

'And yet on the morning tide more trawlers steamed down the river for the fishing grounds, their skippers and crews only too well aware of the hazards, but now perhaps more than ever determined to face them. Their wives and families have had the last two or three days free of the nagging fears which fishermen's people know. Now they will go back to haunting the radio sets, buying the papers, listening to every whisper in the street, desperately anxious for any news of their menfolk and even more concerned that news shall not be such as that which shattered this city today…'

But words, however pungent, however sympathetic, could not disguise the anguish and torment which swept through the fishing community. The loss of one vessel was catastrophic. The loss of three was unimaginable.

As news of the disaster filtered through, families and friends mourned men who would never return, among them a bridegroom-to-be, a man said to have 'fishing fever', a boy who had sailed against the wishes of his parents, a man who had promised his wife just before sailing: 'I will give it up'.

A widow summed it up simply and graphically, reflecting what so many others felt and thought: 'When my man came back tired and exhausted he said he would never go back on trawlers. But like all fishermen he could not give up the sea…all the trawlermen complain about conditions and the food, but they always go back. So did my husband. He told me that no one who has not experienced it for themselves can really know what it is like trawling in the winter. He returned from one trip and told me that one of his mates had an arm torn off in an accident when a giant wave hit the trawler. A long time ago I decided that our two boys were not going to be fishermen.'

And in the churches Hull prayed for its men. In St Wilfrid's Roman Catholic Church 300 people heard Canon Lindy Hall tell them: 'In a world where so much is cheap, false and shoddy, these people are bigger and an inspiration to us all. I think it is a pity the womenfolk have been so often qualified as hysterical and only interested in security for their husbands, brothers, sons and sweethearts. I think it is a pity that a skipper should be classed as callous and the crews looked upon as slap-happy and irresponsible. I think it is a pity that the owners should be qualified as interested only in the financial aspects of fishing. It is unfair because it is so utterly untrue.

'These men are gentlemen in the best sense of the word. These women are worthy of any tribute.

'So many people who do not live here look upon this part of the world as rather uncouth. It is such a pity because there is found here in this fishing community the virtues and values without which no society, whatever it is, can prosper.'

Hull Fish Dock, 5 February 1968

It was not the best day for a meeting.

But the wives had arranged it and were determined to see it through.

For one in particular it was a harrowing occasion. Mrs Christine Smallbone went to meet Mr Mark Hellyer, director of the owners of the *Kingston Peridot*, alongside Yvonne Blenkinsop, Lilian Bilocca and Mary Denness, carrying the terrible shock of knowing that only 10 hours previously her brother Phil Gay had gone down with the trawler he commanded.

During the three-hour meeting Mrs Smallbone broke down and was taken home.

The meeting discussed and reached broad agreement on three key points:

1. Trawlers must report to their base once every 12 hours and if this was not done all efforts should be made to contact them. After a 24 hour silence search and rescue services should be alerted and wives told of the lack of communication.

2. Vessels must have a pre-trip item-by-item check on all safety equipment, the list to be signed only when an inspector was satisfied of its effectiveness.

3. The British Government should commission and build at once at least one mother ship for the fishing fleet to act as a hospital and rescue vessel.

Also present at the meeting were Hull TGWU officers David Shenton, Jack Ashwell and Mike Neve.

It ended amicably with Mr Hellyer telling reporters: 'There was no bitterness at all. The wives of the fishermen have decided they will get for their menfolk what the unions have been unable to obtain up to now. They do not want strike action or anything like that, but they insist something should be done.'

Mrs Bilocca was less diplomatic. As she arrived for the meeting at Hellyers' offices she told the waiting reporters: 'Another one's gone down…more lads have died.' And with tears running down her face she shouted to fishermen who waited near the office: 'Don't go lads. No one gives a damn about you.'

ISAFJORDHUR, ICELAND, 5 FEBRUARY 1968

As *Ross Cleveland* vanished from the radar screens another trawler that night began a battle to survive. She was the Grimsby-based *Notts County* and later, after an escape some would describe as 'miraculous', the crew reflected on the worst hours of their lives, which saw their vessel grounded. One man was killed, having frozen to death in an upturned life raft only yards from safety, and five others, among them Skipper George Burres, were in hospital after a 15-hour ordeal.

Deckhand Frank McGuinness recalled: 'Conditions out there were the worst I have ever seen. The mast was just one block of ice. It was terrifying. Both our radars were knocked out. The *Ross Cleveland* was guiding us to shelter when she went down. We were on our own.'

When the vessel went aground, the Icelanders moved in, the gunboat *Odinn* braving blinding blizzards and mountainous seas to stand by her. Just one mistake and she, too, would have grounded.

Despite the dangers and the intense cold the Icelanders managed to put a lifeboat and dinghies alongside the 441-ton *Notts County* – and take the men off and to hospital in Isafjord where a medical team awaited them.

On the afternoon of 7 February they arrived back in Glasgow where deckhand Gilbert Cook broke the silence of the rest of the crew to tell the whole dramatic story:

'I have been 23 years at sea, never before have I seen anything like this weather. We had been cutting and axing ice formations on the deck and had just stopped for a cup of tea when it happened. The trawler grounded. We did not know where we were because our radar scanners were out of order because of the ice. We had to rely on signals from the trawler *Kingston Emerald*, which was near us and whose radar was working'

Conditions were so bad that no one even knew the direction in which the vessel was sailing.

'Every hand was on deck axing the ice. The blizzard was so thick we could not see the coast or the mountains even after we had grounded. The first thing we did after the ship grounded was to lower a lifeboat and rubber dinghies.'

At the later inquiry into the vessel's loss mate Barry Stokes took up the story: 'I went onto the boat deck and helped the crew to get the starboard raft out. When that was launched I went across to the port side when the ice came down on top of me and injured my ankle. I couldn't stand up so I ordered all the other men to get the rafts ready. I dragged myself along the casing handrails. By this time the skipper came out and told all hands not to leave the ship because he had been in touch with the *Odinn* which would be at the scene within the hour.'

One crewman jumped into the lifeboat, but as he did so it capsized. Desperate efforts were made to rescue him before the raft was washed on board by the wind and sea. Mr Stokes told the inquiry: 'I heard from some of the men that he refused to come out of the raft. He kept telling them "leave me alone" and crawled back in.'

Conditions in the fjord were the worst that deckhand Frank McGuinness, an experienced seaman, had ever seen. 'The mast was just one block of ice. It was terrifying.'

To make matters worse when the vessel hit the rocks its lights and heating went, the ship was in complete darkness until emergency lighting was pressed into service. On the bridge the crew huddled together, shivering with the cold and with fear, with not even enough fresh water available to make themselves a warming drink. And for 15 hours the waiting went on.

Relief came in the form of a tiny raft seen ploughing towards them in seas whipped into creamy foam by the gale. Aboard it were two sailors from the *Odinn*, standing by nearly a mile away. This heroic action by men from a ship which just four years later was to terrorise British fishermen who dared to venture into Icelandic waters during the second Cod War, brought praise from *Notts County* cook Harry Sharpe: 'Those Icelanders were risking death themselves to get us off. The raft could easily have overturned.'

Battling against the elements, the Icelanders managed to inflate two rafts and ferry the men to safety. The ordeal was finally over.

HULL, 26 JANUARY–5 FEBRUARY 1968

As campaigners stepped up their demands for better conditions on trawlers and politicians pondered their next moves, in homes across Hull and the surrounding area families faced up to the terrible reality that men they had loved would never return.

The disasters had highlighted the dangers men faced while at sea. They also threw new light onto the lives of trawlermen when they were ashore. At its heart the tragedy was not only about conditions, it was also about people.

By the nature of his job the fisherman had traditionally led a dislocated family life, spending three quarters of his time away from his wife and family. Three days ashore and back to sea again for another three weeks was the normal procedure in a job which was not so much an occupation, but more a way of life. The blunt truth was that fishermen worked in conditions which would not have been tolerated by shore workers. Never before had this been so clearly highlighted. But it offered little comfort to those who now mourned their men.

Among those missing was a boy who was now mourned by nine brothers and sisters, a man who had promised to give up the sea in two years' time after a lifetime of sailing on trawlers, a young man who had planned to stay at home until March when his wedding was to be held and another making his trip to Iceland purely by chance, having been asked by the skipper to sail earlier than he had planned.

Another man was said to have 'fishing fever', insisting on returning to sea and never missing a trip, and a 15-year-old boy on his first trip, against the wishes of his family.

All were mourned by a community which all too often had been forced to face up to the harsh realities of loss of loved ones at sea.

And as the news filtered through about the conditions on the fishing grounds the nation mourned with Hessle Road. Fifty-nine men were gone. Three ships had sunk. And all in a fortnight.

News of the third tragedy was passed around in a whisper on Hull Fish Dock. Men waiting to sail talked quietly in small groups of the mates they had known. No one said much, perhaps they could not find the words.

The House of Commons, 3.15pm, Monday 5 February 1968

On the famous green leather benches they waited in tense anticipation of the ministerial statement, particularly those members from the great fishing ports of Hull, Grimsby, Fleetwood and Aberdeen. In the fishing communities grief was communal, touching each and every port. On the fishing grounds rivalry was keen, intense at times. In times of loss came unity.

The statement came from Mr J.W.P.Mallalieu, the minister responsible for shipping at the Board of Trade. It was delivered quietly and calmly, without emotion. He told the house that a preliminary inquiry into the loss of the *Ross Cleveland* would be held, followed by a formal investigation. Of her loss he said simply: 'It would be wrong to hold out hope for the crew'. And urgent consideration was being given to what restrictions should be imposed upon the operation of trawlers having regard to their size, the area of operation, the seasons of the year and their stability and freeboard.

James Johnson, the MP for West Hull, whose constituency included the Fish Dock and Hessle Road, told the Commons of the 'numbing despair felt by the people of Hull at this third tragedy in so short a time'. And with his sympathy for the families of the men lost came a plea for a close season for fishing and the setting up of a commission to investigate the industry.

The house listened in silence. For the moment there was no more to be said.

From the *Hull Daily Mail*, Tuesday 6 February 1968

'Britain's fishing industry is facing what could be its biggest ever upheaval. Emotions over the *St Romanus–Kingston Peridot–Ross Cleveland* affair are high. And the shock waves which have hit Hull in the past two weeks are beginning to spread out across the nation.

'The fear, anger and bitterness which is sweeping Hessle Road is beginning to turn into an industrial and political rebellion over safety and working conditions aboard trawlers.

'Between 1948 and 1964 over 750 fishermen died at sea. Figures show that a trawlerman has two and a half times the chance of losing his life at work than a miner. It is this, the death rate and the risks of fishing in mountainous seas and some of the worst weather conditions in the world which have brought the wives of Hessle Road into action.

'Today they are going to London to meet the men who can grant their demands.

'The sincerity of the wives is absolute. They tremble as they address a meeting. Their voices shake and falter. But the sincerity shows all the way.

'The wives, led by 39-year-old Lilian Bilocca were laughed off at first by many in the fishing industry. But now it is accepted that they mean business. What could have turned out to be a hysterical, disorganised protest is now becoming regarded as something of a fighting machine, backed by hundreds.

'There is no doubt that the tragedy has made the trawler people nervous. Women say they live in fear when their men sail. One said she would leave home altogether if her husband made another trip.

'Their men's jobs have been called the most dangerous in Britain. Besides the obvious hazards caused by the weather, a man can be caught against a winch if he loses his footing on a rolling ship, gashed by broken cable, washed overboard and swept away, knocked into the Arctic waters where he will die within four minutes from the cold.

'The dangers are there on every trip. And for facing them a deckhand gets a basic £13 7s a week, plus poundage of £7 per £1,000 on the catch.

'The main questions posed by the loss of the *St Romanus* and *Kingston Peridot* have been those concerning the system of reporting and inclusion of a qualified radio operator. But until the two ships were reported missing, few Hull fisherman had expressed any undue concern.

'Now, however, they are coming round to the women's way of thinking.

'Increasing anger is now being voiced about the hours men work. "Would you work 18 hours in a gale and a blizzard for seven days?" women ask. And another argument is growing over the use of "Christmas crackers" – men who are taken on at Christmas time and who do not normally sail.

'At the moment the men are content to follow the women's lead. They certainly back the wives in any action they propose. When the campaign for better conditions began fears were expressed that extremist elements would seize the opportunity to make political capital out of the whole affair. But so far this has not been the case. The wives are united. They know the course they are taking. Any outside intervention would be quickly crushed.

'The wives are militant and determined. "When women make up their minds about anything, it takes Heaven and earth to shift 'em," said one deckhand.

'And so the battle moves into gear. The echoes from Hull's worst trawler tragedy in living memory are likely to be heard around St Andrew's Dock for a very long time to come.'

THE MINISTRY OF AGRICULTURE, LONDON, 6 FEBRUARY 1968

It was the moment the campaigning wives of Hull had fought for and prayed for.

They left a city in mourning on the 8.55 train – and left behind one of the delegation who should have joined them.

Not with the party which arrived for a meeting with the Minister of Agriculture, Mr Fred Peart, and The Minister of State at the Board of Trade,

Mr J.P.W. Mallalieu was Mrs Christine Smallbone. She stayed at home to grieve for her brother, Philip Gay, the skipper of the *Ross Cleveland*.

For Lilian Bilocca, Yvonne Blenkinsop and Mary Denness the meeting was a magnificent achievement. The campaign launched on the streets and terraces around Hessle Road had won over the hearts and minds of some of the most powerful people in Britain.

The result of the meeting, which lasted 110 minutes – a series of proposals which would bring revolutionary new measures for safety at sea.

These included a recommendation that trawler owners should keep vessels away from Iceland in extreme weather, tighter regulations on reporting procedures for vessels at sea, a suggestion that a mother ship sail with the British fleet providing hospital, rescue and weather forecast services and safety checks on trawlers' equipment before vessels sailed.

It was, said Mrs Bilocca, the happiest moment of her life. Mrs Denness told the pack of pressmen awaiting the delegation as it left the ministry: 'Three women have achieved more in one day than anything that has ever been done in the trawler industry in 60 years.'

HULL DAILY MAIL NEWSROOM, TUESDAY 6 FEBRUARY 1968

At the end of a rough day Charles Levitt at last began to relax. The tension was by now getting to most of his staff directly involved in the disaster. Reporters had spent days and nights on the Fish Dock and around the Hessle Road area and were tired to the point of exhaustion. He, too, was feeling the strain. It is often claimed that being news editor is the single most difficult job on any newspaper. The situation had helped underline the conjecture as fact.

Just after 4.30pm the room was at last quiet as the staff had, for the most part, left. Levitt tidied his desk, made brief notes in the margin of a copy of that night's paper relating to stories which needed to be followed up the following day and checked the diary entries. In the heat of the moment the other news must not be forgotten either.

The *Mail's* coverage of the disaster had been brilliantly organised, the paper priding itself on having the most detailed and certainly the most accurate reports of a situation which now saw every national newspaper with a team of reporters based in Hull. TV stations and national BBC radio too threw staff and equipment into the city. In its hour of mourning Hull was under siege from the media.

In the days when regional TV had only started to make any sort of impact on the early evening schedules and when local radio was still but a figment of a BBC man's imagination the local paper remained the supreme conveyor of news of any matter of local interest, however insignificant. On a major issue such as the loss of three trawlers and 58 men the *Mail* was, as always, Hull's daily 'Bible' with over 390,000 readers every evening. Five editions of the paper carried the news to the city and surrounding county areas every day, the last one, distributed only in central, Hull finally rolling off the presses at 5.05pm.

When the newsdesk phone rang at 4.40 that afternoon no one could possibly have anticipated the impact, not only on the newspaper, but on the city and then the world.

The message was brief but undeniably sensational. A survivor had been found alive in Iceland from the lost Hull trawler *Ross Cleveland.*

There was no time for deep thought. Within seconds the late duty sub editor was pressed into instant service to write the headline, the story was dictated to a linotype operator and minutes later the front page had been ripped apart, it now carried the banner headline 'Trawler disaster survivor found alive' .

HARRY EDDOM'S HOME, COTTINGHAM NEAR HULL, TUESDAY 6 FEBRUARY 1968

The grey telephone in the hallway rang and broke the silence of mourning.

Reporters and cameramen were there to record the moment that Rita Eddom spoke to the husband she believed to be dead. In a six-minute call made from his hospital bed in Isafjord, taken by Rita at 6.40pm, Eddom simply told her: 'The ship's gone down and all my mates have gone.'

Reporters scribbled busily in notebooks as Mrs Eddom, crying and twice breaking down, bombarded her husband with questions: 'Harry, is it you? I can't believe it…I can't… Are you all right? What happened? When are you coming back? Are you going back to sea?'

In the early hours of the following day Mrs Eddom left Cottingham to board a plane for Iceland, accompanied by her young brother Dennis and Mr Eddom's brother, Michael, and parents.

On leaving the hospital after an emotional reunion she was to tell reporters: 'I was half afraid to see Harry. I felt it would be like seeing a ghost.'

The Press were there before her, many of them dashing to Iceland in chartered planes as soon as the news broke.

And at Glasgow reporters and photographers were joined by radio broadcasters as Mrs Eddom and her family boarded the plane. She told them: 'All my life I have seen the menfolk come home for a few days and then be off to sea again. I knew exactly what sort of a life I could expect when I married Harry. I have no regrets. There is such pride among trawlermen and women feel this pride.'

ABBOTSINCH AIRPORT, GLASGOW, 7 FEBRUARY 1968

Sixteen crewmen from the Grimsby trawler *Notts County* came home from an ordeal none would ever forget. As they stepped from the aircraft their thoughts were with two men they had left behind in hospital, Skipper George Burres and mate Barry Stokes. There were memories, too, of a third man who died as he scrambled to float a life raft.

One crewman, John Davidson, of Sheffield, told a national newspaper: 'We had to use our hands like picks to hack the ice away and get onto the rafts. I'm not religious, you know, but that night I prayed "Please God let me see my little lad again."'

LONDON, 8 FEBRUARY 1968

The Government wasted no time once it began to appreciate the full implications of the disaster. Trawler owners, skippers and trade union officials were among 50 delegates from 16 organisations who gathered at the Board of Trade.

It was a meeting which was to have far-reaching effects. The Government agreed that all British trawlers should be withdrawn from the Isafjord area until a naval vessel or modern freezer trawler which could provide support facilities was on station.

ISAFJORD, ICELAND, 9 FEBRUARY 1968

A half-laughing, half-crying Rita Eddom ran into the arms of the husband she had believed dead. Tears streamed down her face as she hugged him.

As she left, flashguns blinded her and other members of Eddom's family, and television cameras recorded every second. It was a furore which angered Dr Ulfur Gunnerssonn who told an Icelandic newspaper: 'I have never seen anything like this. We have had so much disturbance that we have had to postpone several operations. Journalists and cameramen were co-operative individually, but when they got together they lost control and some violated the sanctuary of the hospital.'

THE ROYAL STATION HOTEL, HULL, 15 FEBRUARY 1968

From late afternoon the place was packed with journalists from newspapers, radio and television. Cables snaked across carpets, cameras were lined up before a table. Journalists chatted and smoked as they waited.

Shortly after 8pm the moment they had gathered here for finally arrived. Harry Eddom came home to Hull.

Hours earlier he had landed in Glasgow and then travelled south by car – complete with a police escort.

Once at the hotel, where he arrived at 7.45pm, he was given a brief medical examination by the medical officer to the Hull trawling industry and then put before photographers for just three minutes. Reporters were given five minutes, the room silent as Eddom told more of his story. Earlier it had been agreed by pressmen that only one journalist would ask questions. It was brief, to the point and final. After that last interview Harry Eddom was to remain silent until his full story was told at the official inquiry into the *Ross Cleveland*'s loss.

Eleven weeks after returning home Eddom left for the fishing grounds again, departing from St Andrew's Dock on the 661-ton *Ross Antares* under Skipper Gordon Jopling. His wife said: 'At the bottom of my heart I always knew he would go back and I would not really stop him.'

THE MAN WHO CAME BACK FROM THE DEAD

From a report by Dr Lewis Pugh prepared for the British Medical Journal and later given as evidence to the formal inquiry into the loss of *Ross Cleveland*:

'The men sat on the sides of the [life] raft and baled out the water with one man's seaboots. One entrance was torn, the other incompletely closed...C [the youngest survivor] was shivering violently and soon began to fail. A [Eddom] rubbed and smacked his limbs to try to keep him warm, while B [the vessel's bosun] went on bailing. At last there was only a little water left, perhaps 4 inches [10 centimetres] slopping about. C gradually lost consciousness and slipped down onto the floor of the raft. They laid him on the thwarts, but he soon died. Death occurred within one to one and a half hours of boarding the raft. B soon began to fail, too. His speech was slurred and incoherent and he gradually lost consciousness. He died one to two hours after C.'

From an interview with Harry Eddom, March 1968, by Sub Lt H.J. Matthews, Surg-Cmdr D.E. Mackay and Surg-Cmdr J.F. Ryan:

'Eddom eventually felt the raft ground on some rocks. His hands felt numb, but otherwise his condition was good. His thighs felt cold and ached a little. He clambered out and pulled the raft containing the bodies of his two shipmates, clear of the water line and then scrambled clear of the rocks. He knew he was in a bay or fjord and, when he looked around, he could see lights across the water so he decided to walk round the bay.

'The raft had gone about six miles downwind, a surprisingly short distance in the weather conditions.

'Before starting his walk Eddom, who was wet through to his skin, decided to take his stockings off to wring them but, after coping with one he did not attempt the other because it was difficult to remove his thigh boots with his cold hands. He made his way for eight to nine miles through snow during the short daylight hours to the head of the farmhouse and thought the worst was over. On approaching closely, however, he found it was deserted and he failed in his attempts to break in. [In fact it was a house shut up for winter].'

Throughout the night Eddom remained on the lee side of the building, not daring to sit down for fear of falling asleep, but shivering violently and intermittently. In the morning, from the cold dim dawn of an Arctic winter, came salvation.

'He saw a young lad tending sheep nearby and he managed to attract attention after some difficulty as his voice was weak. He was supported and half carried because he was unable to walk properly owing to numb feet. His hands were now so swollen that the two rings he wore could not be seen…

'Mr Eddom is a level-headed, phlegmatic individual aged about 30, of stocky build about 5ft 4ins in height and an estimated 11 stone; he does not carry much fat…he withstood two classic dangers, immersion hypothermia and so-called exposure. His plastic 'duck suit' which he bought himself for £7, undoubtedly saved his life.'

Evidence of Harry Eddom to the inquiry into the loss of the *Ross Cleveland*, October 1968:

'We just laid over to port and never came back. When we took the first sea he [Skipper Gay] put her at full speed but she made no attempt to get back and piled more water on top. She just piled more water on top of the water we had had and never attempted to come back up or anything. We were going full, but she never attempted to come back up. The wheel was hard to starboard.

'I was jammed against the telegraph and said "Come on, we don't want to be here now" and we went along the casing after getting out through the starboard door of the bridge. They were getting the raft, the bosun and Barry Rogers and some others. I could not see whether the skipper came out.

'As the life raft was inflated she threw me into the water.'

The next thing he knew he was pulled into the raft.

The trawler's port side was under water and the port life rafts could not be reached.

'She swilled me to the after end of the ship where they were getting the raft out and Barry Rogers pulled me in. The bosun had on a jersey, a pair of trousers and wellington boots. Barry Rogers had a T-shirt, a pair of John L's and I don't think he had any boots on. We closed one end of the life raft but the other end had got torn and we could not close that.'

He was practically swilled out of the water-filled raft trying to launch a flare. They then tried to bale out with a canister.

'I was awake all the time we were on the raft. I saw nothing more of the *Ross Cleveland* after we got into the raft. I had no idea where it was we came ashore, none at all.'

He dragged the life raft up the beach as far as he could.

'I saw a light and I just walked round the shore until I got to a farmhouse. There was no one in it. I stood behind that until daylight the next morning. This was when the lad found me. I just kept dozing and had no proper sleep. The lad found me and took me to his farmhouse and then they took me round by ship to Isafjord.'

HOLY TRINITY CHURCH, HULL, FRIDAY 8 MARCH 1968

The lone tenor bell boomed out its dismal message over the rooftops of the Old Town, the sound being borne on a light spring breeze towards the Humber.

They gathered just before 3pm to remember husbands, fathers, sons and friends who would never return.

In the great church over 800 people in all struggled with their emotions as they honoured their dead.

The church itself was a mass of colour from the scores of bouquets and wreaths placed there by families and friends. Each bore a simple, moving message…'to a darling husband'…'to my daddy'…'to our dear son'.

Outside, huge silent crowds watched as the mourners arrived for what was to be one of Hull's most poignant hours.

In the church stifled sobbing broke the intensity of the silence as staff of the Royal National Mission to Deep Sea Fishermen rose to read the names of the dead and then to pray for all seafarers.

In one corner of the vast, soaring church, a dark-suited fisherman bowed his head and remembered. His name was Harry Eddom.

The Bishop of Hull, the Rt Revd Hubert Higgs, in a brief address dug deep into the heart of the tragedy, reflecting on its repercussions. Nothing, he said, should be spared which could humanely make the fisherman's job more endurable and safe from foreseeable dangers. In such matters the Government, the public and all concerned with the fishing industry had a duty to the men involved.

It was a view shared fully throughout Hull.

THE SERVICE IN MEMORY OF THOSE WHO LOST THEIR LIVES IN THE HULL TRAWLERS ST ROMANUS, KINGSTON PERIDOT, ROSS CLEVELAND, HOLY TRINITY CHURCH, KINGSTON UPON HULL, FRIDAY 8 MARCH 1968, AT 3PM.

Order of service

All stand for the hymn

Rock of Ages, cleft for me,

Let me hide myself in thee;

Let the water and the blood,

From thy riven side which flowed,

Be of sin the double cure:

Cleanse me from its guilt and power.

Not the labours of my hands

Can fulfil thy laws' demands;

Could my zeal no respite know,

Could my tears for ever flow.

All for sin could not atone:

Thou must save, and thou alone.

Nothing in my hand I bring,

Simply to thy Cross I cling;

Naked, come to thee for dress;

Helpless, look to thee for grace;

Foul, I to the mountain fly;

Wash me, Saviour, or I die.

While I draw this fleeting breath,

When my eyelids close in death,

When I soar through tracts unknown,

See thee on thy judgement throne;

Rock of ages, cleft for me,

Let me hide myself in thee.

Then shall the Minister say, all still standing

The eternal God is thy refuge, and underneath are the everlasting arms. Neither death, nor life, nor angels, nor principalities, nor powers, nor things present, nor things to come, nor height, nor depth, nor any other creature shall be able to separate us from the love of God, which is in Jesus Christ our Lord.

The Congregation will kneel for prayer

Minister: Almighty God, unto whom all hearts be open, all desires known, and from whom no secrets are hid: Cleanse the thoughts of our hearts by the inspiration of thy Holy Spirit, that we may perfectly love thee, and worthily magnify thy Holy Name; through Christ our Lord. Amen.

All: Our Father, which art in Heaven, Hallowed be thy name, thy Kingdom come; Thy will be done in earth as it is in heaven. Give us this day our daily bread; And forgive us our trespasses, as we forgive them that trespass against us; And lead us not into temptation; But deliver us from evil. For thine is the Kingdom, the power and the glory, for ever and ever. Amen.

All sit for the lesson read by Skipper Laurie Oliver OBE
Revelation 21, verses 1–7

'Then I saw a new heaven and a new earth; for the first heaven and the first earth had passed away, and the sea was no more. And I saw the holy city, new Jerusalem, coming down out of heaven from God, prepared as a bride adorned for her husband; and I heard a great voice from the throne saying, 'Behold, the dwelling of God is with men. He will dwell with them, and they shall be his people, and God himself will be with them; he will wipe away every tear from their eyes, and death shall be no more, neither shall there be mourning nor crying nor pain any more, for the former things have passed away."

'And he who sat upon the throne said, "Behold I make all things new." Also he said, "Write this for these words are trustworthy and true." And he said to me, "It is done! I am the Alpha and the Omega, the beginning and the end. To the thirsty I will give water without price from the fountain of the water of life. He who conquers shall have this heritage, and I will be his God and he shall be my son."'

All stand for the hymn

Lead us heavenly Father, lead us
O'er the world's tempestuous sea;
Guard us, guide us, keep us, feed us,
For we have no help but thee;
Yet possessing every blessing,
If our God our father be.
Saviour, breathe forgiveness o'er us:
All our weakness thou dost know;
Thou didst tread this earth before us,
Thou didst feel its keenest woe;
Lone and dreary, faint and weary
Through the desert thou didst go.

Spirit of our God descending,
Fill our hearts with heavenly joy,
Love with every passion blending,
Pleasure that can never cloy:
Thus provided, pardoned, guided,
Nothing can our peace destroy.

All kneeling, the minister shall say

Let us remember in silence and in gratitude those who lost their lives in the Hull trawlers *St Romanus, Kingston Peridot* and *Ross Cleveland.*

After the silence the names who lost their lives will be read by the staff of the Royal National Mission to Deep Sea Fishermen and the Fishermen's Bethel. The prayers will be said by Anglican, Free Church and Roman Catholic representatives.

Those who lost their lives in the *St Romanus*

James Wheeldon, Raymond Mearns, Kenneth Suffling, Cyril Ashton, Alan Nicholas, John Walker-Roberts, John Brooks, Herbert Pye, Terence Walton, Alan Court-Bohan, David Redfern, John Williams, Robert Dockerty, George Rutter, Melvyn Williams, John Hutchinson, Walter Snaddon, Brian Wilson, Ronald Jackson, David Stott.

Almighty God, Father of all mercies and giver of all comfort: deal graciously we pray thee, with those who mourn, that casting every care on thee, they may know the consolation of thy love, through Jesus Christ our Lord. Amen.

Those who lost their lives in the *Kingston Peridot*

Raymond Wilson, William Heelas, George Rose, Adam Ali, Martin Larsen, Peter Smith, Charles Blanchard, Leonard Ledingham, Robert Smith, Eugene Carney, George Matfin, Kenneth Swaine, Henry Fowler, Peter McGowan, David Warley, Stephen Giblin, Henry Riches, Enoch Watson, Alfred Hartley, Robert Rivett.

Almighty God, Father of all mercies and giver of all comfort: deal graciously we pray thee, with those who mourn, that casting every care on thee, they may know the consolation of thy love; through Jesus Christ our Lord. Amen.

Those who lost their lives in the *Ross Cleveland*

Philip Gay, Keith Hookem, Maurice Petman, Michael Barnes, George Keal, Barry Rogers, Kenneth Brandtman, George Ketley, Frederick Sawdon, Douglas Hairsine, Dennis Mayes, Maurice Swain, Alan Harper, James McCracken, Rowland Thomson, Walter Hewitt, Michael Morris, Trevor Thomson.

Almighty God, Father of all mercies and giver of all comfort: deal graciously, we pray thee, with those who mourn, that casting every care on thee, they may know the consolation of thy love; through Jesus Christ our Lord. Amen.

All kneeling the minister shall say

Let us pray for all seafarers.

Almighty God, whose way is in the sea and whose paths are in the great waters: Be present we beseech thee, with our brethren in the manifold dangers of the deep; protect them from all perils, prosper them in their course and bring them in safety to the haven where they would be, with a grateful sense of Thy mercies; through Jesus Christ our Lord. Amen.

Let us give thanks for all God's mercies, remembering especially the survival of Harry Eddom, the mate of the *Ross Cleveland*.

Almighty God, Father of all mercies, we give thee most humble and hearty thanks for all thy goodness and loving kindness. And we beseech thee, give us such a sense of all thy mercies that our hearts may be truly thankful; through Jesus Christ our Lord. Amen.

All say together

The grace of our Lord Jesus Christ and the love of God, and the fellowship of the Holy Spirit, be with us all evermore. Amen.

All stand for the hymn

The Lord's my shepherd, I'll not want;
He makes me down to lie
In pastures green; he leadeth me
The quiet waters by.

My soul he doth restore again
And me to walk doth make
Within the paths of righteousness
E'en for his own Name's sake.

Yea though I walk through death's dark vale
Yet I will fear none ill;
For thou art with me and thy rod
And staff me comfort still.

My table thou hast furnished

In presence of my foes;

My head thou dost with oil anoint

And my cup overflows.

Goodness and mercy all my life

Shall surely follow me

And in God's house for evermore

My dwelling place shall be.

All sit for

The address by the Bishop of Hull.

All stand for the hymn

Eternal Father, strong to save,

Whose arm hath bound the restless wave,

Who bidd'st the mighty ocean deep

Its own appointed limits keep:

O hear us when we cry to thee

For those in peril on the sea.

O Christ, whose voice the water heard

And hushed their raging at thy word,

Who walkedst on the foaming deep,

And calm amid the storm didst sleep:

O hear us when we cry to thee

For those in peril on the sea.

O Holy Spirit, who didst brood
Upon the waters dark and rude,
And bid their angry tumult cease
And give, for wild confusion, peace:
O hear us when we cry to thee
For those in peril on the sea.

All kneel for
The Blessing.

All remain kneeling and sing as a prayer
O Trinity of love and power,
Our brethren shield in danger's hour;
From rock and tempest, fire and foe,
Protect them whereso'er they go:
Thus ever more shall rise to thee
Glad hymns of praise from land and sea.

THE VICTORIA GALLERIES, HULL CITY HALL, 9 OCTOBER 1968

In the dignified calm of a formal hearing Judge John Naisby and assessors R.A. Beattie and W.F. Wright began the first of three hearings into the loss of the vessels. The first was into the disappearance of *St Romanus. Kingston Peridot* followed and finally came the drama of the *Ross Cleveland* with evidence from its sole survivor.

The inquiries were thorough and far reaching, technical and at times highly emotional. This was the last formal act in a tragedy which had engulfed an entire community.

The findings came three weeks after the first inquiry had begun. The court found that *St Romanus* was in all respects seaworthy but it could not find what caused her loss. There was, however, no evidence to suggest that it was due to the wrongful act or default of anyone.

One mystery surrounding the loss was never adequately explained – the mystery message picked up by the Icelandic trawler *Vikingur III* on 11 January. The incident was 'open to some doubt' according to the inquiry findings.

The court added: 'All the members of the court gained the impression that the first mate of the vessel was endeavouring to tell the truth, but his recollection in its entirety cannot have been correct. In the first place it was impossible for *St Romanus* to have been anywhere near the position stated by him and although it is not beyond the bounds of possibility that there should be some freak atmospheric conditions obtaining there were many shore stations permanently manned on the distress frequency and a good number of other ships which must have been nearer to *St Romanus* than *Vikingur III*…no trace has been found of any such station or ship having received any Mayday message about that time.'

The court also took up the question of radio operators being carried on fishing vessels, a question which had been at the heart of the wives' campaign. The official report said: 'It was the habit of the owners of the *St Romanus* to provide on board their trawlers a qualified radio officer whenever possible. The evidence established that at the time when the *St Romanus* sailed no such officer was available and in accordance with the agreement with the union an extra deckhand was shipped.

'The evidence clearly established the value of a radio officer…in the view of the court a radio officer should be carried whenever possible and consideration might well be given to the problem as to how to increase the supply of radio officers willing to sail on trawlers.'

Kingston Peridot was found to be fit for a voyage to Iceland waters under normal conditions likely to be encountered there. But, the court found, her stability was insufficient to stand up to the relatively exceptional occurrence of a combination of winds of storm or hurricane force with corresponding sea conditions and a substantial period of heavy ice formation on her superstructure.

The loss of the vessel was not found to have been caused or contributed to by the wrongful act or default of anyone.

The same finding applied to *Ross Cleveland*. From information available to the court she was fit to sail to Icelandic waters but was unable to withstand a relatively exceptional combination of winds of hurricane force with corresponding sea conditions, even in the shelter of a fjord, and a prolonged period of heavy ice formation on her superstructure.

The hearing also produced the following suggestion for the future safety of fishermen:

'It is clear from the evidence in these three inquiries that it is of the utmost importance that the owners and builders of trawlers should co-operate wholeheartedly with the Board of Trade on questions affecting the safety of trawlers and that no one should delay or sit back when any question affecting the safety of trawlers and their crews at sea is raised and rely upon someone else to take the initiative. There was evidence of some such co-operation in the past, but there was also further evidence that it had not always taken place. Furthermore, in the opinion of the court it has been demonstrated that there is a need for all parties to the fishing industry, owners and builders of trawlers and of skippers and crews, to play their part in making what must be a hazardous occupation as safe as possible.'

The dangers facing fishermen were also uppermost of Admiral Sir Derec Holland-Martin, who headed the Committee of Inquiry into Trawler Safety, set up in March that year and which, in an interim report published on 27 September, recommended an experimental weather advisory and communications service be operated as an experiment that winter from a ship at sea in the area north of Iceland.

Two months later, on 29 November, the fishing fleet's first 'mother' ship, the Hull trawler *Orsino* under Skipper Ted Wooldridge, sailed from St Andrew's Dock. Conversion work included extra accommodation for specialist personnel and the creation of a small hospital and room for additional equipment. Aboard was a weather advisory officer.

The lessons had been learned. The price of fish had been far too high.